THE COMPLETE BOOK OF
SPANISH
GRADES 1-3

AMERICAN
EDUCATION
PUBLISHING™

An imprint of Carson-Dellosa Publishing LLC
Greensboro, North Carolina

American Education Publishing™
An imprint of Carson-Dellosa Publishing LLC
P.O. Box 35665
Greensboro, NC 27425 USA

Printed in the U.S.A.   All rights reserved.   ISBN 978-0-7696-8564-9

06-028131151

Table of Contents

My Spanish Book

Me llamo _____

Numbers

uno

dos

tres

cuatro

cinco

The Complete Book of Spanish

Numbers

seis

siete

ocho

nueve

diez

Numbers 1–5

Say each word out loud.

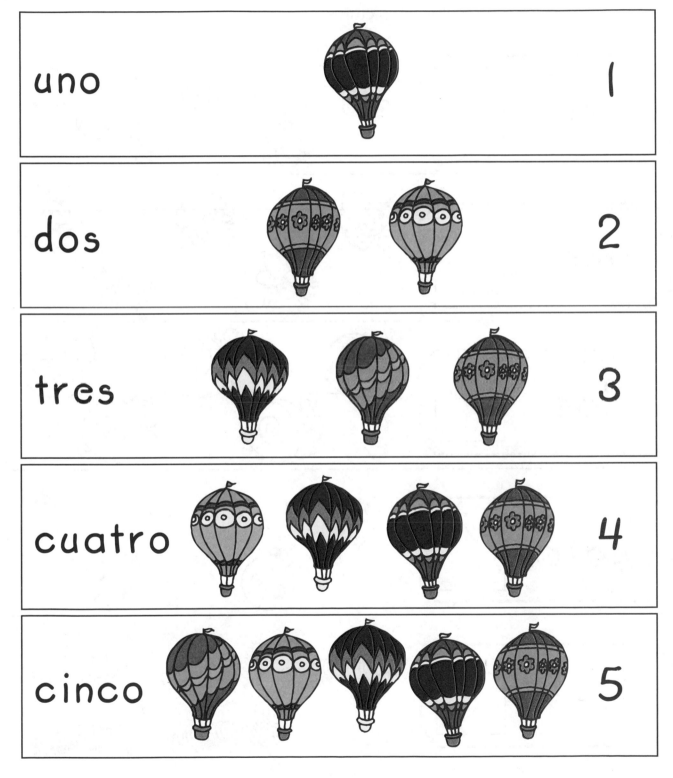

uno — 1

dos — 2

tres — 3

cuatro — 4

cinco — 5

The Complete Book of Spanish

Nombre_____

Numbers Review

Write the number next to the Spanish word. Circle the correct number of animals for each number shown. Then, color the pictures.

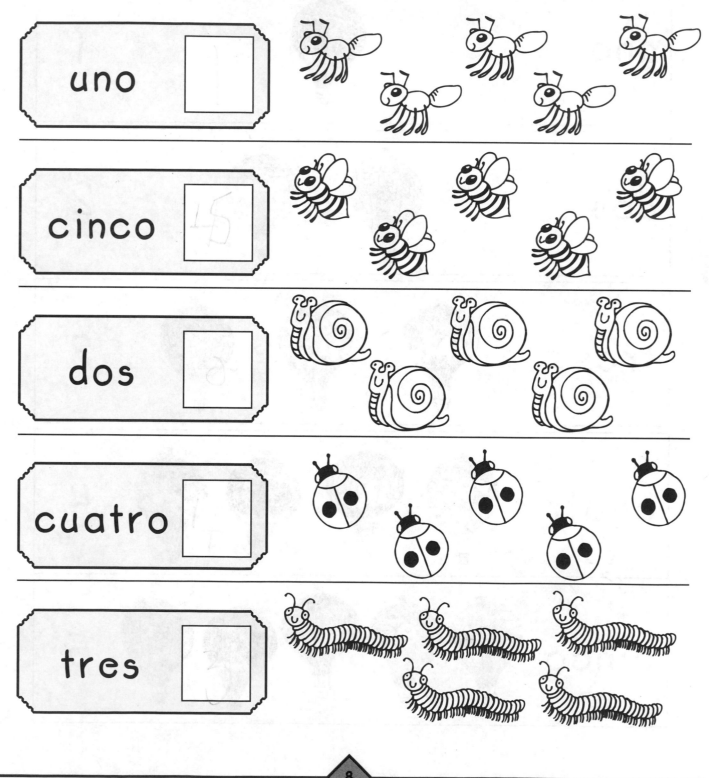

uno	
cinco	45
dos	
cuatro	
tres	

Matching Numbers

Draw a line from the word to the correct picture. Then, color the pictures.

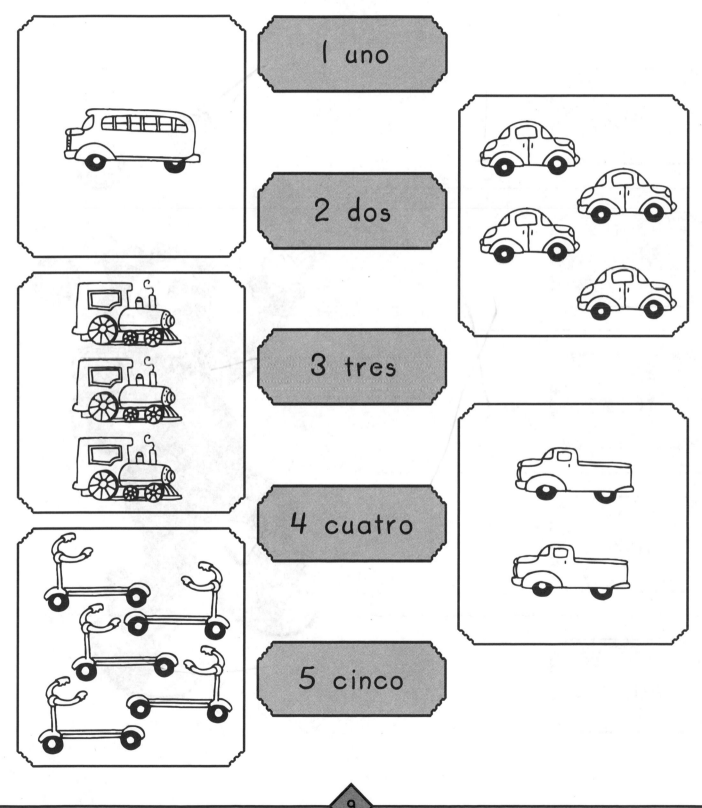

The Complete Book of Spanish

Nombre_____

Number the Stars

Draw the correct number of stars next to each number.

uno

dos

tres

cuatro

cinco

1–10 Matching

Draw a line to match each object to the number that is written in Spanish.

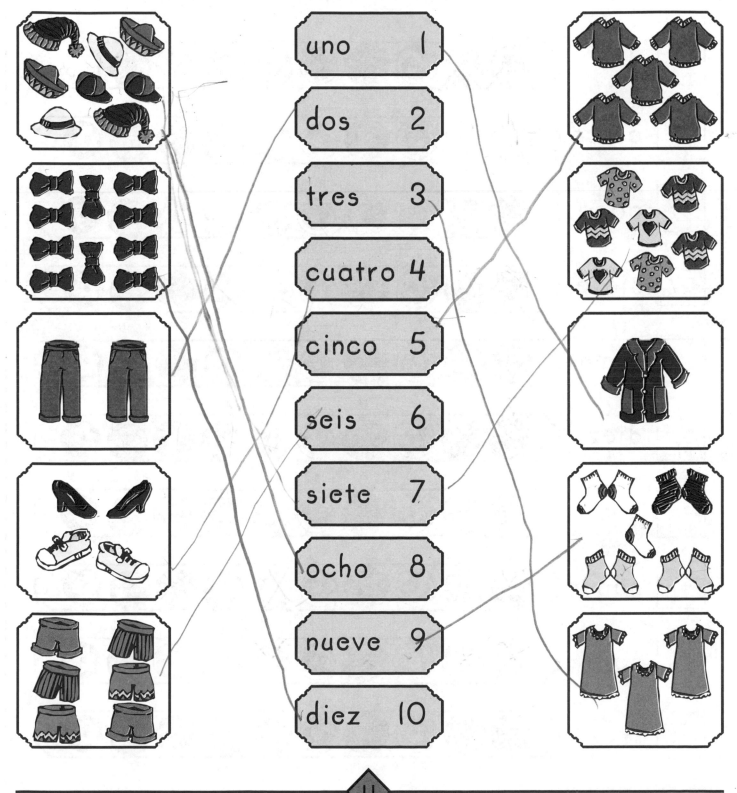

uno   1

dos   2

tres   3

cuatro 4

cinco   5

seis   6

siete   7

ocho   8

nueve   9

diez   10

The Complete Book of Spanish

Nombre_____

Count the Cookies

In each box at the left, write the number that matches the Spanish word. Cross out the correct number of cookies to show the number written in Spanish. The first one is done for you.

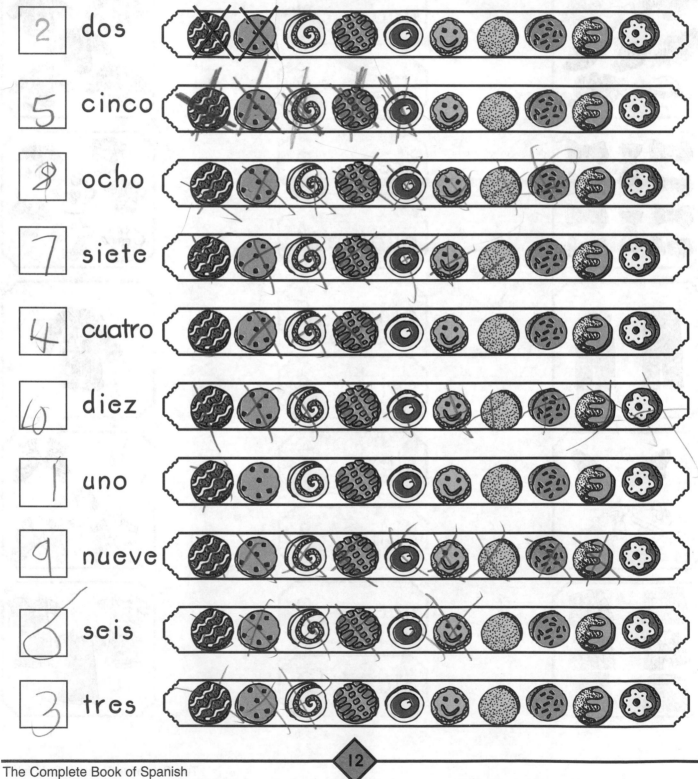

2	dos
5	cinco
8	ocho
7	siete
4	cuatro
10	diez
1	uno
9	nueve
6	seis
3	tres

The Complete Book of Spanish

My Favorite Number

Write your favorite number from 1 to 10 in the boxes. Draw a picture to show that number.

My favorite number is ⌐toes¬ .

In Spanish it is called ⌐diez¬ .

Circles 1–10

Draw the correct number of circles in each box.

uno	1
dos	2
tres	3
cuatro	4
cinco	5

seis	6
siete	7
ocho	8
nueve	9
diez	10

Coloring 0–10

Color or circle the number of butterflies that shows the number written in Spanish.

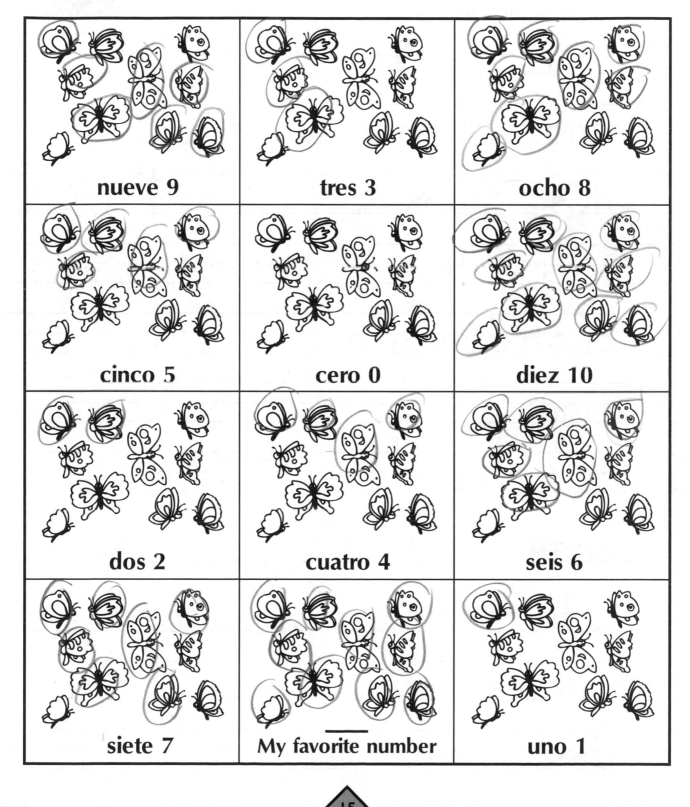

nueve 9	tres 3	ocho 8
cinco 5	cero 0	diez 10
dos 2	cuatro 4	seis 6
siete 7	____ My favorite number	uno 1

The Complete Book of Spanish

Numbers 0–10

Trace, then write each of the number words from 0 to 10 in Spanish.
Use the words at the left to help you.

0   cero   cero   cero   cero

1   uno   uno   uno uno

2   dos   dos   dos dos dos

3   tres   tres   tres tres

4   cuatro   cuatro   cuatro

5   cinco   cinco   cinco

6   seis   seis   seis seis sis

7   siete   siete   siete sixta

8   ocho   ocho   ocho ocho

9   nueve   nueve   nueve nueve

10   diez   diez   diez dejz

The Complete Book of Spanish

Numbers 0–10

Say each word out loud. Circle the number that tells the meaning of the word.

seis	5	0	(6)
ocho	1	9	(8)
uno	3	(1)	8
cero	8	10	(0)
siete	9	(7)	1
tres	0	(3)	5
diez	(10)	8	7
nueve	4	2	(9)
cuatro	7	5	(4)
dos	(2)	6	3
cinco	6	4	(5)

The Complete Book of Spanish

Nombre_____

Dot-to-Dot

Connect the dots. Start with the Spanish word for one and stop at ten. What shape did you get? _____

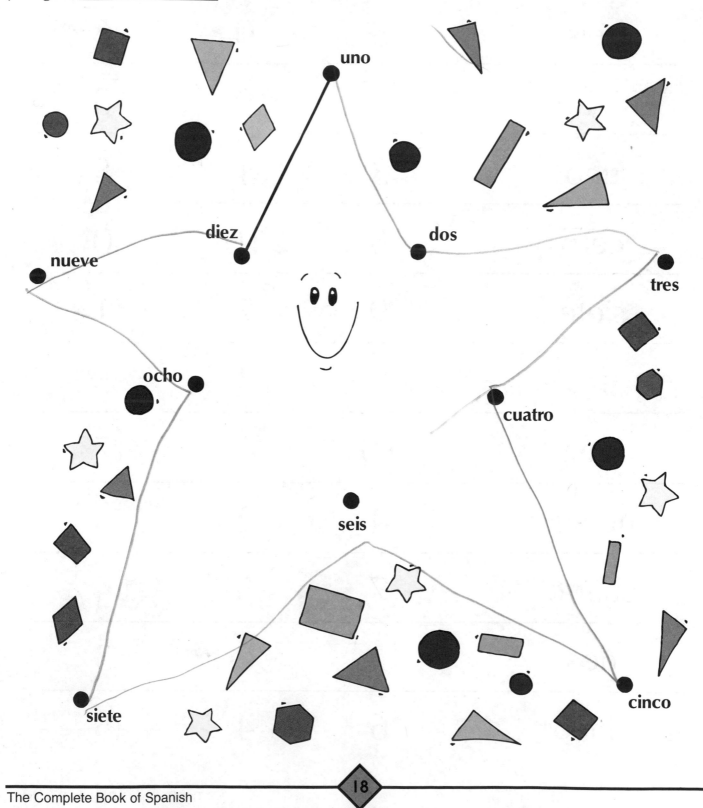

The Complete Book of Spanish

Numbers 0–20

In the left column, write the number words from 0 to 10 in Spanish. Use the words in the box below to help you. Then, in the second column, write the numbers beside each Spanish word. Examples are done for you.

0 cero

1 _____

2 _____

3 _____

4 _____

5 _____

6 _____

7 _____

8 _____

9 _____

10 _____

_____11_____ once

_____ doce

_____ trece

_____ catorce

_____ quince

_____ dieciséis

_____ diecisiete

_____ dieciocho

_____ diecinueve

_____ veinte

siete	ocho	uno	seis	nueve
cero	cinco	dos	cuatro	diez	tres

Now, count from 1 to 20 in Spanish. Point to the numbers as you say them.

1 **2** **3** **4** **5** **6** **7** **8** **9** **10**
11 **12** **13** **14** **15** **16** **17** **18** **19** **20**

The Complete Book of Spanish

Show Your Numbers

In each box, write the number for the word written. Then, draw and color pictures that show the numbers.

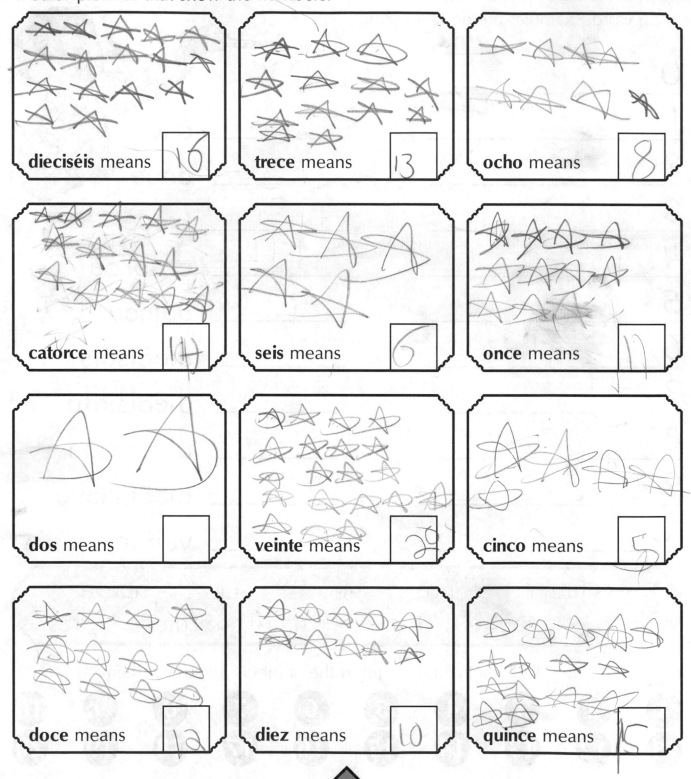

dieciséis means　16

trece means　13

ocho means　8

catorce means　14

seis means　6

once means　11

dos means

veinte means　20

cinco means　5

doce means　12

diez means　10

quince means　15

20

Sunshine 0–20

Write the number for each Spanish word. Cross out the correct number of suns to show the number written in Spanish. The first is done for you.

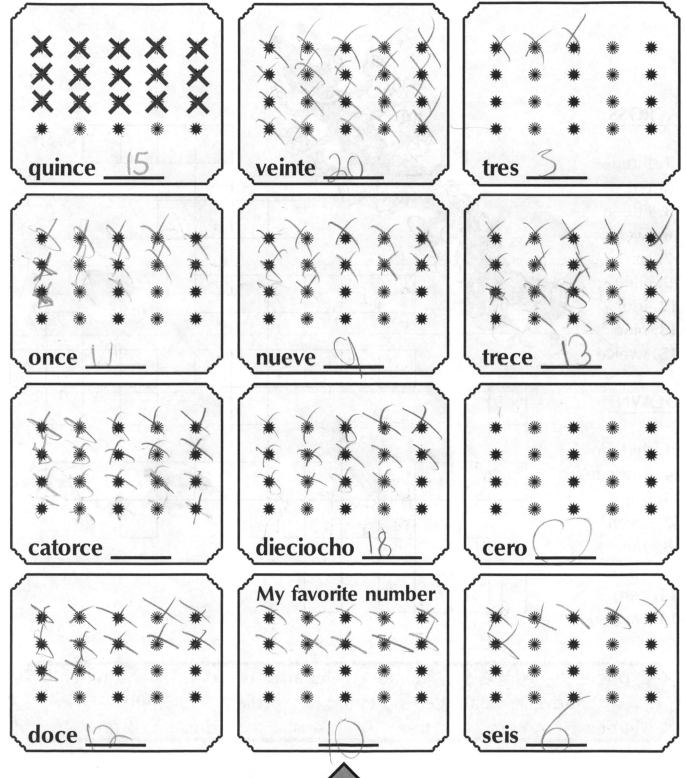

quince 15

veinte 20

tres 3

once 11

nueve 9

trece 13

catorce ____

dieciocho 18

cero ____

doce 12

My favorite number 10

seis 6

The Complete Book of Spanish

Numbers Crossword

Use the words at the bottom to help you with this crossword puzzle. Write the Spanish number words in the puzzle spaces. Follow the English clues.

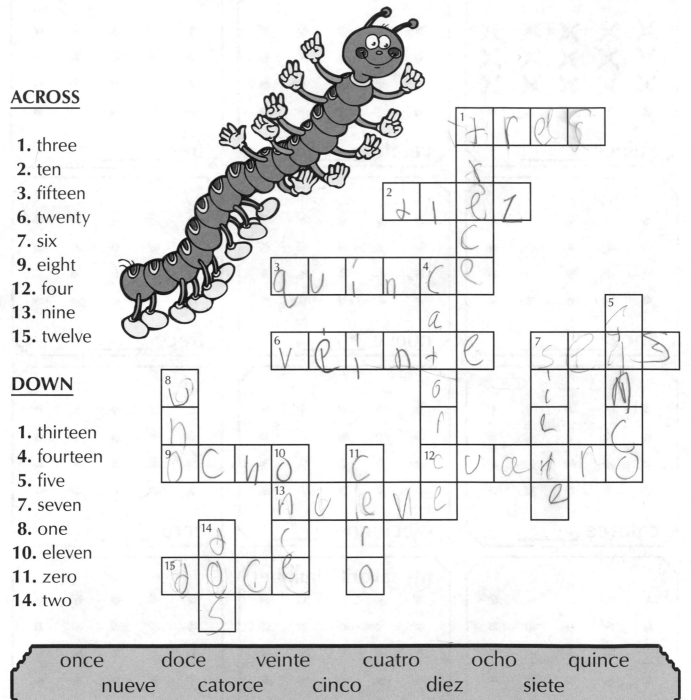

ACROSS

1. three
2. ten
3. fifteen
6. twenty
7. six
9. eight
12. four
13. nine
15. twelve

DOWN

1. thirteen
4. fourteen
5. five
7. seven
8. one
10. eleven
11. zero
14. two

once   doce   veinte   cuatro   ocho   quince
nueve   catorce   cinco   diez   siete
trece   cero   tres   seis   dos   uno

Nombre _____

Numbers

After each numeral, write the number word in Spanish. Refer to the words below to help you.

Word Bank

veinte	cuatro	nueve	diez	diecisiete	quince
doce	once	trece	siete	uno	tres
catorce	dos	cero	ocho	cinco	dieciséis
diecinueve		dieciocho		seis	

---

0 _cero_

1 _uno_

2 _dos_

3 _tres_

4 _cuatro_

5 _cinco_

6 _seis_

7 _siete_

8 _ocho_

9 _nueve_

10 _diez_

11 _once_

12 _doce_

13 _trece_

14 _catorce_

15 _quince_

16 _dreisate_

17 _diecisiete_

18 _dieocho_

19 _diecinueve_

20 _veinte_

Numbers Illustration

Write the number. Draw that many things in the box. The first one is done for you.

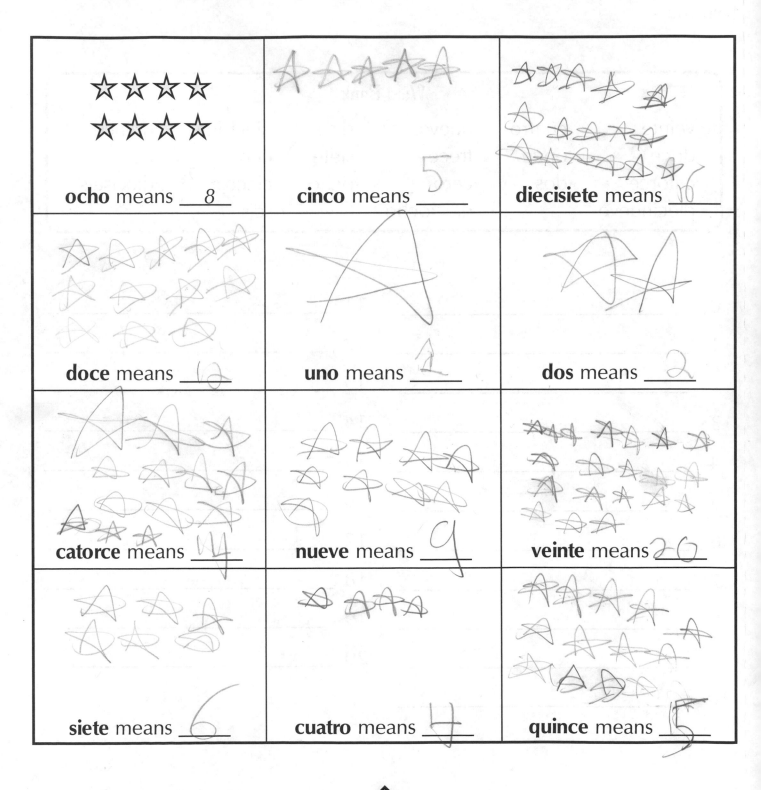

ocho means __8__   cinco means __5__   diecisiete means __16__

doce means __12__   uno means __1__   dos means __2__

catorce means __14__   nueve means __9__   veinte means __20__

siete means __6__   cuatro means __4__   quince means __15__

The Complete Book of Spanish

Nombre_____

Number Puzzle

Write the English number words in the puzzle spaces. Follow the Spanish clues.

Word Bank

one	eight	eleven	seventeen
two	nine	thirteen	eighteen
six	ten	fourteen	twenty

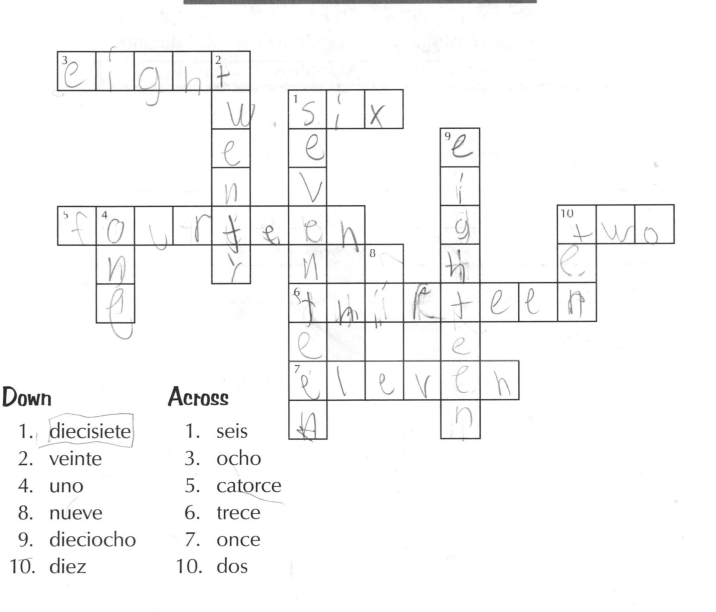

Down

1. diecisiete
2. veinte
4. uno
8. nueve
9. dieciocho
10. diez

Across

1. seis
3. ocho
5. catorce
6. trece
7. once
10. dos

The Complete Book of Spanish

Counting On

Follow a pattern to write the numbers from 21–29. Change *veinte* (20) to *veinti* and add the number words from *uno* to *nueve*. (Watch for accent marks on *dos, tres,* and *seis*.)

Rewrite the number words in the Word Bank in order.

Word Bank

veintiséis	veinticinco	treinta	veintiocho
veintidós	veintiuno	veintinueve	veinticuatro
	veintisiete	veintitrés	

21 veintiuno
22 veintidos
23 veintitres
24 veintiquatro
25 vienticinco

26 vientiseis
27 vientisiete
28 vientiocho
29 veintiquatro
30 treinta

Complete the pattern to write the numbers from 31–39. Use the word *y* to join *treinta* (30) with the number words *uno* to *nueve*.

30 treinta
31 treintauno
32 treintatos
33 treinta tres
34 treinta quatro

35 treinta sinco
36 treintaseis
37 treintaseite
38 treintaocho
39 treinta cuatro

Nombre_____

Number Find

Circle the Spanish number words that you find in the word search. Then write the English meaning of each word.

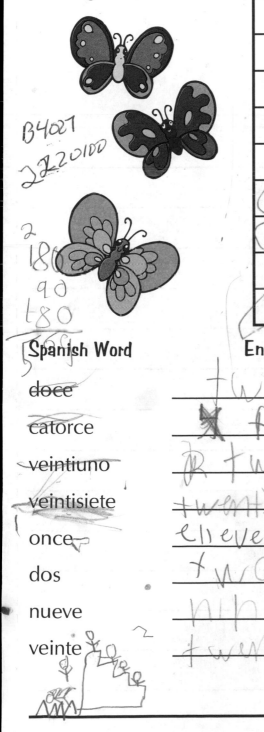

d	u	e	t	e	i	s	o	d	n	e	e
t	o	a	i	z	l	h	i	u	c	v	t
r	v	c	t	j	c	e	e	a	h	l	e
e	j	e	e	o	c	v	t	u	i	h	i
s	t	p	i	i	e	o	g	n	e	e	s
b	i	r	o	n	r	v	p	q	m	c	i
z	t	c	e	c	t	m	t	c	s	n	t
e	h	a	e	i	c	i	v	h	o	i	n
o	v	p	z	s	n	i	d	e	d	u	i
e	t	n	i	e	v	t	n	ó	c	q	e
s	e	i	s	a	z	o	a	c	s	n	v
v	e	i	n	t	i	u	n	o	o	c	o

Spanish Word	English	Spanish Word	English
doce	twelve	treinta	thirty
catorce	fourteen	siete	seven
veintiuno	twenty one	ocho	eight
veintisiete	twenty seven	veintidós	twenty two
once	eleven	cinco	five
dos	two	seis	six
nueve	nine	quince	fifteen
veinte	twenty	tres	three
		dieciocho	eighteen

27

The Complete Book of Spanish

Counting by Tens

The Spanish numbers ten, twenty, thirty, forty, and fifty are written out of order below. Write the value of each number word in the blank.

____ treinta   ____ cincuenta   ____ cuarenta

____ diez   ____ veinte

Write the numbers from 30–59 in Spanish.

30 Treinta

31 Treinta unoe

32 treinta dose

33 treinta tres

34 treinta quatro

35 treinta sinco

36 treinta seis

37 Treinta sire

38 Treinta ocho

39 treinta nueve

40 cuarenta

41 cuarenta uno

42 cuareta dos

43 cuareta tres

44 cuareta quatro

45 cuarenta sinco

46 cuarenta seise

47 cuarenta seata

48 cuarenta ocho

49 cuarenta nueva

50 cincuenta

51 cincuenta uno

52 cincuenta dos

53 cincuenta tres

54 cincuenta quatro

55 cincueta cinco

56 cincueta seis

57 cincu eta seita

58 cincueta ocho

59 cincueta nueve

28

Number Search

Circle the Spanish number words that you find in the word search. Write the English meanings at the bottom of the page next to the Spanish words from the puzzle.

c	s	c	r	i	w	d	v	k	z	r	e	t
r	i	y	e	u	g	m	l	e	k	v	r	k
e	i	n	i	r	y	q	i	q	e	e	s	g
o	y	p	c	a	o	d	c	u	c	i	y	p
d	y	t	f	o	t	u	n	e	e	y	i	d
r	l	z	i	w	a	n	e	s	o	t	c	o
s	r	q	o	r	c	v	e	c	e	n	w	n
o	g	h	e	u	e	z	s	u	n	c	c	u
d	c	n	a	i	a	j	r	i	c	i	o	e
o	t	t	n	r	n	k	x	s	e	n	u	d
a	r	t	v	n	u	n	l	i	e	t	i	q
o	e	b	a	t	n	i	e	r	t	r	e	c
c	a	t	o	r	c	e	u	e	e	d	t	h

Spanish Word	English	Spanish Word	English
cero	zero	dos	two
cuatro	four	seis	six
ocho	eight	diez	tene
doce	twelve	catorce	fourteen
veinte	twenty	cuarenta	fourty
uno	one	tres	three
cinco	five	siete	seven
nueve	nine	once	eleven
trece	thirteen	quince	fifteen
treinta	thirty	cincuenta	first

29

Spanish Alphabet

EL ABECEDARIO (EL ALFABETO) EN ESPAÑOL

Aa	a	Jj	jota	Rr	ere
Bb	be	Kk	ka	Ss	ese
Cc	ce	Ll	ele	Tt	te
CHch	che	LLll	elle	Uu	u
Dd	de	Mm	eme	Vv	ve
Ee	e	Nn	ene	Ww	doble u
Ff	efe	Ññ	eñe	Xx	equis
Gg	ge	Oo	o	Yy	i griega
Hh	hache	Pp	pe	Zz	zeta
Ii	i	Qq	cu		

Rhyming Vowel Practice

Say these sentences out loud:

A, E, I, O U, ¡Más sabe el burro que tú!

A, E, I, O, U, ¿Cuántos años tienes tú?

Listening Practice

Say the Spanish word for each number out loud.
Write the first letter of the words you hear.

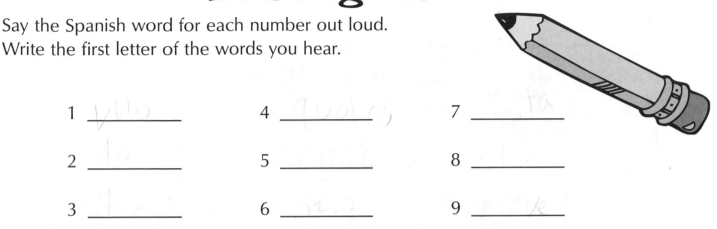

1 _____ 4 _____ 7 _____

2 _____ 5 _____ 8 _____

3 _____ 6 _____ 9 _____

Color the letters of the Spanish alphabet. Say them in Spanish as you color them.

A B C D E F G

H I J K L M N

Ñ O P Q R S T

U V W X Y Z

The Alphabet

El abecedario (the alphabet)

a	a	**h**	hache	**n**	ene	**t**	te
b	be	**i**	i	**ñ**	eñe	**u**	u
c	ce	**j**	jota	**o**	o	**v**	ve
ch	che	**k**	ka	**p**	pe	**w**	doble u
d	de	**l**	ele	**q**	cu	**x**	equis
e	e	**ll**	elle	**r**	ere	**y**	i griega
f	efe	**m**	eme	**s**	ese	**z**	zeta
g	ge						

Listening Practice

Write each letter of the alphabet as you say it out loud.

1. _a_
2. _be_
3. _ce_
4. _che_
5. _te_
6. _e_
7. _efe_
8. _de_
9. _hache_
10. _i_
11. _jota_
12. _ka_
13. _ele_
14. _elle_
15. _eme_
16. _eme_
17. _eñe_
18. _o_
19. _pe_
20. _cu_
21. _ere_
22. _ese_
23. _te_
24. _v_
25. _u_
26. _doble u_
27. _equis_
28. _i griega_
29. _zeta_

Nombre_____

The Alphabet

El abecedario (the alphabet)

a	a	**j**	jota	**r**	ere
b	be	**k**	ka	**s**	ese
c	ce	**l**	ele	**t**	te
ch	che	**ll**	elle	**u**	u
d	de	**m**	eme	**v**	ve
e	e	**n**	ene	**w**	doble u
f	efe	**ñ**	eñe	**x**	equis
g	ge	**o**	o	**y**	i griega
h	hache	**p**	pe	**z**	zeta
i	i	**q**	cu		

Listening Practice

Write the Spanish word for each number below. Then, spell each word out loud.

1 uno

2 dose

3 tres

4 quatro

5 cinco

6 seis

7 seite

8 ocho

9 neueve

10 deise

11 once

12 dose

13 tresy

14 quaterce

15 quincia

16 deisete

The Complete Book of Spanish

Nombre_____

Parts of Speech

tú

usted

pretty

bonita

ugly

feo

Parts of Speech

happy

alegre

to read

leer

sad

triste

to play

jugar

to eat

comer

Using You

Spanish uses two different forms of the pronoun *you*.

Tú is used when talking to

1. someone you refer to by a first name.
2. your sister, brother, or cousin.
3. a classmate.
4. a close friend.
5. a child younger than yourself.

usted

Usted (*Ud.*) is used when talking to

1. someone with a title.
2. an older person.
3. a stranger.
4. a person of authority.

Write the names of 6 or more people in each box below.

Use **tú** when you are talking to . . .	Use **usted** when you are talking to . . .
• refer are first name • a sister brother o cousin • a clos freind • a clas mate • a child younger than • a child odare than	• some one important • some one with authorit • some one title • a stranger • an old pearse • a teacher

Picking Pronouns

Spanish uses two different forms of the pronoun *you*.

Tú is used when talking to

1. someone you refer to by a first name.
2. your sister, brother, or cousin.
3. a classmate.
4. a close friend.
5. a child younger than yourself.

Usted (Ud.) is used when talking to

1. someone with a title.
2. an older person.
3. a stranger.
4. a person of authority.

Explain to whom you might be talking and what you are asking in each question.

¿Cómo te llamas tú?_____child_____

¿Cómo se llama usted?____a Stranger_____

¿Cómo estás tú?_____close freind_____

¿Cómo está usted?____asome pers with title_____

¿Cuántos años tienes tú?____child younger than_____

¿Cuántos años tiene usted? ____old Pearson_____

Who Is It?

Write the names of people you may know that fit each description below.

tú–informal or familiar form of you	
someone you refer to by first name	
your sister or brother (or cousin)	
a classmate	
a close friend	
a child younger than yourself	

usted–formal or polite form of you	
someone with a title	
an older person	
a stranger	
a person of authority	

How would you speak to each person below? Write tú or usted after each person named.

1. Dr. Hackett _____

2. Susana _____

3. a four-year-old _____

4. your grandfather _____

5. the governor _____

6. your best friend _____

7. your sister _____

8. the principal _____

9. a classmate _____

10. a stranger _____

Masculine and Feminine

All Spanish nouns and adjectives have gender. This means they are either masculine or feminine. Here are two basic rules to help determine the gender of words. There are other rules for gender which you will learn as you study more Spanish.

1. Spanish words ending in -o are usually masculine.
2. Spanish words ending in -a are usually feminine.

Write the following words in the charts to determine their gender. Write the English meanings to the right. Use a Spanish-English dictionary if you need help.

maestra	libro	escritorio	negro	abrigo	sopa	tienda
amigo	ventana	pluma	maestro	vestido	fruta	museo
silla	puerta	anaranjado	amiga	camisa	queso	casa
rojo	cuaderno	blanco	falda	chaqueta		

Masculine		Feminine	
words ending in -o	meaning of the word	words ending in -a	meaning of the word

More Than One

Spanish nouns can be placed into two groups—singular nouns (one of something) or plural nouns (more than one of something). Nouns that end in –s are usually plural. Nouns ending in other letters are usually singular.

Read the following familiar nouns. Write **S** if the noun is singular and **P** if the noun is plural.

_____ 1. calcetines   _____ 2. dedo   _____ 3. botas

_____ 4. cuerpo   _____ 5. vegetales   _____ 6. ciudad

_____ 7. escuela   _____ 8. sandalias   _____ 9. zapatos

_____ 10. guantes   _____ 11. casa   _____ 12. boca

Follow these rules to write the following Spanish words in the plural.

1. If the word ends in a vowel, add -s.
2. If the word ends in a consonant, add -es.
3. If the word ends in z, change the z to c before adding -es.

1. carne _____   6. nariz _____

2. silla _____   7. abrigo _____

3. ciudad _____   8. señor _____

4. lápiz _____   9. borrador _____

5. azul _____   10. pollo _____

The Complete Book of Spanish

Nombre_____

More and More

Write the plural form of each Spanish clue word in the puzzle.

Across

1. hombro
4. falda
5. zapato
7. museo
8. nariz
10. gato
11. sombrero
13. oso
14. lápiz

Down

2. borrador
3. vaso
6. escuela
9. casa
12. mesa

Nombre_____

It's a Small World

In Spanish, there are four ways to say "the"—*el, la, los,* and *las.* The definite article (the) agrees with its noun in gender (masculine or feminine) and number (singular or plural).

Masculine singular nouns go with *el.* Feminine singular nouns go with *la.*

Examples: *el libro* (the book)   *el papel* (the paper)
la silla (the chair)   *la regla* (the ruler)

Masculine plural nouns go with *los.* Feminine plural nouns go with *las.*

Examples: *los libros* (the books)   *los papeles* (the papers)
las sillas (the chairs)   *las reglas* (the rulers)

Refer to the Word Bank to complete the chart. Write the singular and plural forms and the correct definite articles. The first ones have been done for you.

Word Bank				
cuaderno	mesa	pluma	oso	falda
papel	gato	bota	silla	libro

English	Masculine Singular	Masculine Plural
the book	el libro	los libros
the paper		
the notebook		
the cat		
the bear		

English	Feminine Singular	Feminine Plural
the chair	la silla	las sillas
the table		
the boot		
the skirt		
the pen		

One or Some

In English, the words *a, an,* and *some* are indefinite articles. In Spanish, there are four indefinite articles—*un, una, unas,* and *unos.*

Masculine singular nouns go with *un.* Feminine singular nouns go with *una.*

Examples: *un libro* (a book)   *una silla* (a chair)
                 un papel (a paper)   *una mesa* (a table)

Masculine plural nouns go with *unos.* Feminine plural nouns go with *unas.*

Examples: *unos libros* (some books)   *unas sillas* (some chairs)
                 unos papeles (some papers)   *unas mesas* (some tables)

Refer to the Word Bank to complete the chart. Write the singular and plural forms and the correct indefinite articles. The first one has been done for you.

Word Bank				
cuaderno	mesa	pluma	oso	falda
papel	gato	bota	silla	libro

English	Masculine Singular	Masculine Plural
a book	*un libro*	*unos libros*
a paper		
a notebook		
a cat		
a bear		

English	Feminine Singular	Feminine Plural
a chair		
a table		
a boot		
a skirt		
a pen		

43

Nombre_____

Watch How Many

Refer to the given articles and nouns to translate the following phrases into Spanish. Use a Spanish-English dictionary if you need help.

Articles

un	una	unos	unas
el	la	los	las

Nouns

cine (m)	dedo	elefantes (m)	museo	tijeras
cara	cuerpo	borradores (m)	agua	cuadernos
blusa	falda	cucharas	boca	caballos
				camas

1. a skirt _____

2. the body _____

3. the spoons _____

4. the mouth _____

5. the elephants _____

6. some scissors _____

7. the finger _____

8. a museum _____

9. the face _____

10. a blouse _____

11. the horses _____

12. some notebooks _____

13. the beds _____

14. a movie theater _____

Nombre_____

Pretty Colors

Adjectives are words that tell about or describe nouns. Color each box as indicated in Spanish. Use a Spanish-English dictionary if you need help.

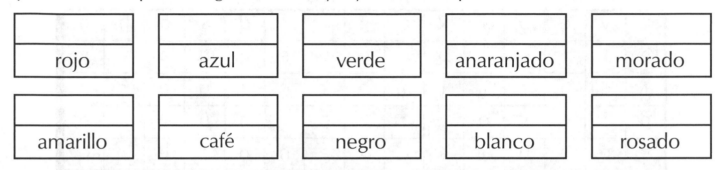

rojo	azul	verde	anaranjado	morado
amarillo	café	negro	blanco	rosado

Here are some new adjectives. Copy the Spanish adjectives in the boxes. Write the Spanish words next to the English at the bottom of the page.

bonita	pretty	feo	ugly
grande	big	pequeño	small
limpio	clean	sucio	dirty
viejo	old	nuevo	new
alegre	happy	triste	sad

old _____   pretty _____   sad _____

big _____   small _____   happy _____

new _____   dirty _____   ugly _____

clean _____

Abundant Adjectives

Circle the Spanish words you find in the word search. Then, write the English meanings next to the Spanish words at the bottom of the page.

v	v	é	o	i	x	q	g	r	r	d	s	a	h	o
e	i	f	o	l	b	p	q	u	s	e	n	a	v	y
r	e	a	r	r	l	m	b	k	n	a	q	e	r	a
d	j	c	s	o	g	i	h	o	r	n	u	y	b	d
e	o	r	b	i	s	e	r	a	n	n	f	h	i	o
y	x	o	x	b	n	a	n	a	a	i	c	h	c	q
t	t	l	v	v	x	j	d	l	m	l	t	x	b	j
l	o	o	o	p	a	o	c	o	i	a	e	o	i	o
l	l	c	i	d	ñ	e	k	m	d	m	l	g	y	e
v	m	e	o	e	o	e	o	e	h	o	p	w	r	f
n	h	d	u	c	d	r	t	l	l	k	i	i	y	e
i	b	q	n	n	a	s	j	n	r	z	s	c	o	z
u	e	a	a	d	i	y	g	r	t	x	m	b	u	z
p	l	r	o	r	d	f	u	b	f	o	j	o	r	s
b	g	s	t	v	u	k	v	y	v	s	l	u	z	a

rojo _____ café _____ azul _____

limpio _____ feo _____ sucio _____

pequeño _____ viejo _____ negro _____

amarillo _____ anaranjado _____ triste _____

grande _____ blanco _____ rosado _____

morado _____ nuevo _____ verde _____

alegre _____ bonito _____

Words to Describe

Descriptive adjectives are words that describe nouns. Refer to the Word Bank to write the Spanish adjective that describes each picture.

Word Bank

alegre	grande	nuevo	pequeño	feo	rico
limpio	sucio	bonita	triste	viejo	pobre
alto	bajo	abierto	cerrado		

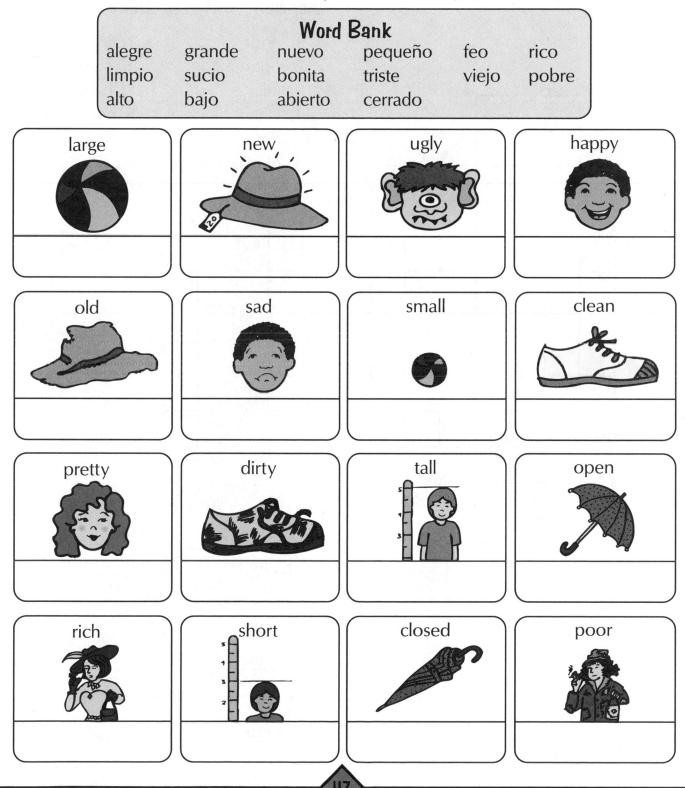

large	new	ugly	happy
old	sad	small	clean
pretty	dirty	tall	open
rich	short	closed	poor

47

Nombre _____

Words to Describe

Write the Spanish words for the clue words in the crossword puzzle.

Across

3. poor
7. open
9. tall
11. clean
12. dirty
13. new

Down

1. ugly
2. closed
4. happy
5. pretty
6. large
8. old
10. sad

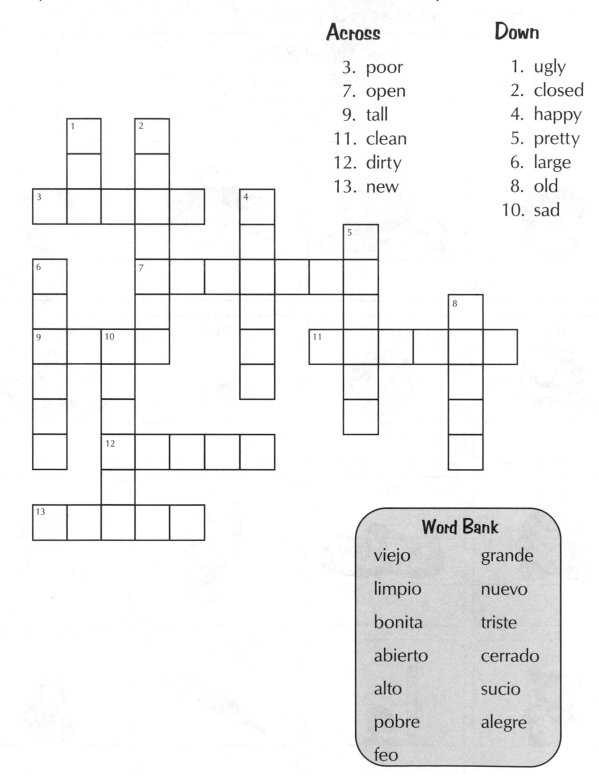

Word Bank

viejo	grande
limpio	nuevo
bonita	triste
abierto	cerrado
alto	sucio
pobre	alegre
feo	

Nombre _____

Open and Close

Would you know what to do if your teacher told you to do something in Spanish? In each box, copy the Spanish word. Then, write the English word below it from the Word Bank.

corten		cierren	
_____		_____	
_____		_____	
peguen		levántense	
_____		_____	
_____		_____	
pinten		siéntense	
_____		_____	
_____		_____	
canten		párense	
_____		_____	
_____		_____	
abran		dibujen	
_____		_____	
_____		_____	

Word Bank

sing	sit down	close	glue	open
stop	cut	paint	stand up	draw

49

The Complete Book of Spanish

Write It Down

Write the Spanish word for each clue in the crossword puzzle.

Across

3. paint
4. open
7. stand up
8. sing
9. paste
10. cut

Down

1. draw
2. sit down
5. close
6. stop

Word Bank

canten	corten	levántense
párense	cierren	abran
siéntense	pinten	dibujen
	peguen	

See It, Say It

On your turn roll the die, move your marker, and give the command in Spanish.

• If you can't remember a Spanish word, ask for help and skip a turn.

• The winner is the first player to reach the finish.

• For two to four players.

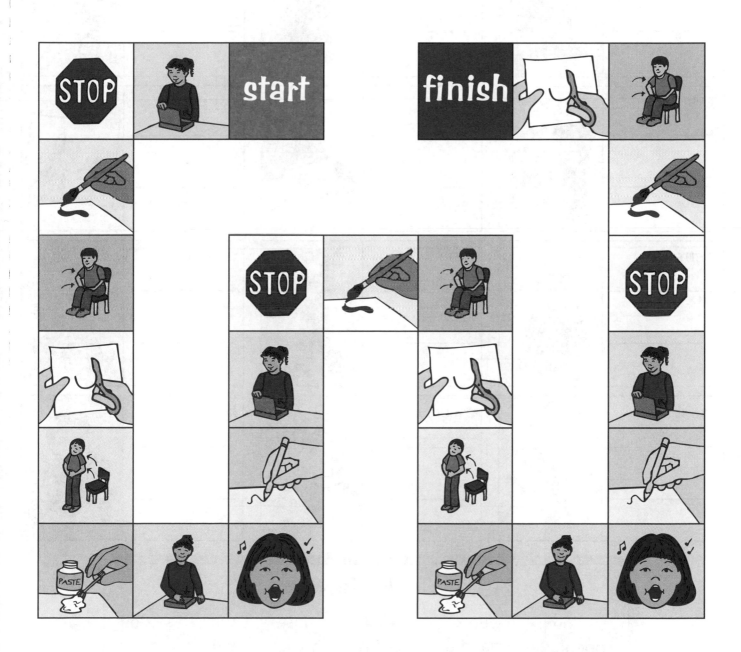

The Complete Book of Spanish

Simon Says

Would you know what to do if your teacher asked you to do something in Spanish?
In each box, copy the Spanish word then write the English meaning below it.

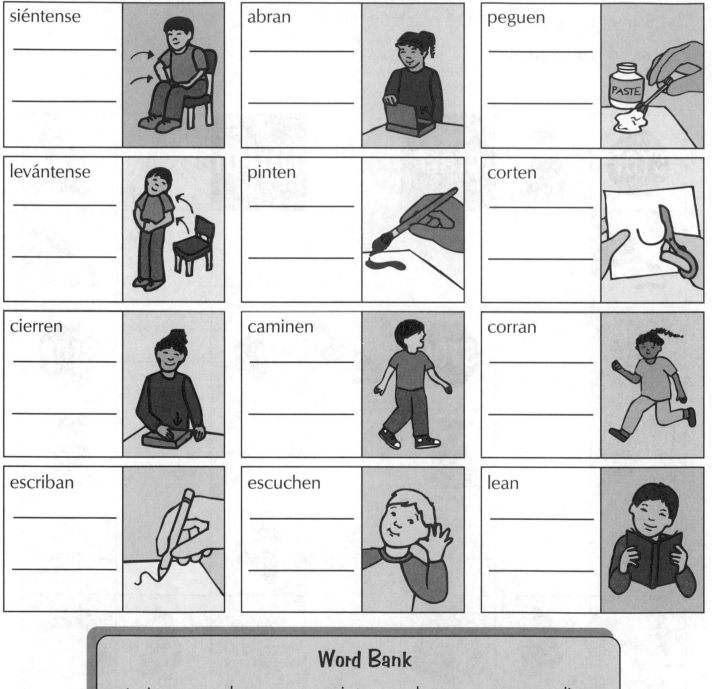

siéntense

levántense

cierren

escriban

abran

pinten

caminen

escuchen

peguen

corten

corran

lean

Word Bank

| sit down | glue | paint | close | run | listen |
| open | stand up | cut | walk | write | read |

Search and Find

Circle the Spanish words you find in the word search. Write the English meanings at the bottom of the page next to the Spanish words from the puzzle.

n	l	p	p	u	m	d	o	c	n	a	n	n	p	v
j	g	a	j	n	a	v	o	e	s	e	e	j	i	o
b	t	v	g	r	c	r	l	i	n	j	e	l	n	l
e	f	b	o	f	r	i	é	i	u	b	o	x	t	t
p	s	k	a	a	a	n	m	b	a	j	m	d	e	e
e	c	n	n	b	t	a	i	n	r	o	h	r	n	e
g	n	b	e	e	c	d	c	c	x	u	p	n	x	n
u	r	c	n	t	b	n	t	a	o	i	j	a	n	s
e	m	s	e	h	n	r	n	e	n	r	g	e	r	e
n	e	i	y	x	j	á	i	e	s	t	t	l	o	i
y	t	g	o	l	c	q	v	n	r	n	e	e	p	m
r	n	r	n	h	c	m	e	e	q	r	e	n	n	b
a	b	r	a	n	t	u	p	k	l	u	e	r	e	r
o	y	p	n	e	h	c	u	c	s	e	e	i	a	w
x	u	n	u	n	a	b	i	r	c	s	e	n	c	p

Spanish Word	English	Spanish Word	English
corten	_____	corran	_____
levántense	_____	escriban	_____
peguen	_____	abran	_____
siéntense	_____	escuchen	_____
caminen	_____	cierren	_____
pinten	_____	lean	_____

The Complete Book of Spanish

Action Words

In each box, copy the Spanish action verbs. Then, write the English word below it.

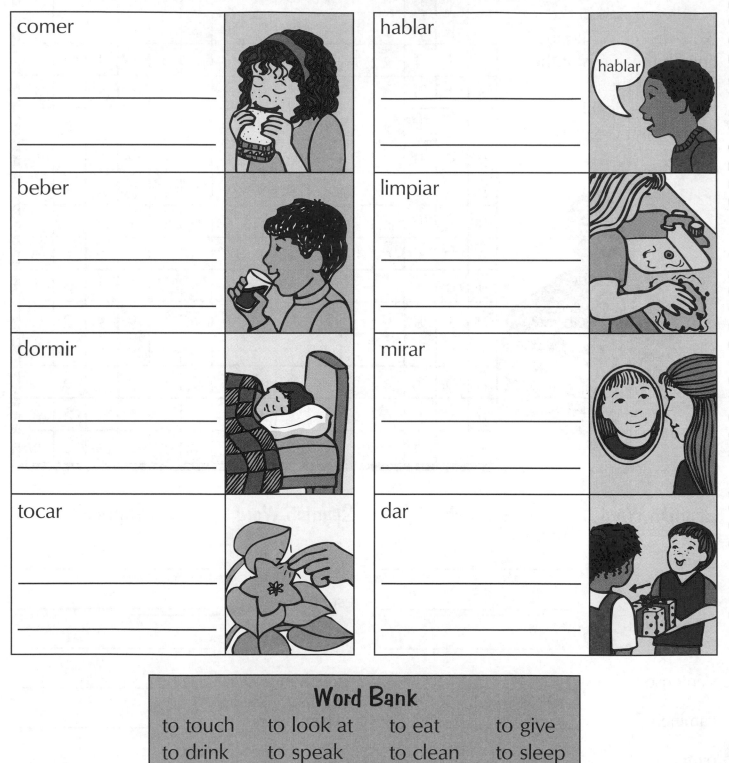

comer

_____

_____

hablar

_____

_____

beber

_____

_____

limpiar

_____

_____

dormir

_____

_____

mirar

_____

_____

tocar

_____

_____

dar

_____

_____

Word Bank

to touch	to look at	to eat	to give
to drink	to speak	to clean	to sleep

Action Figures

Write the Spanish words from the Word Bank that fit in these word blocks. Write the English below the blocks.

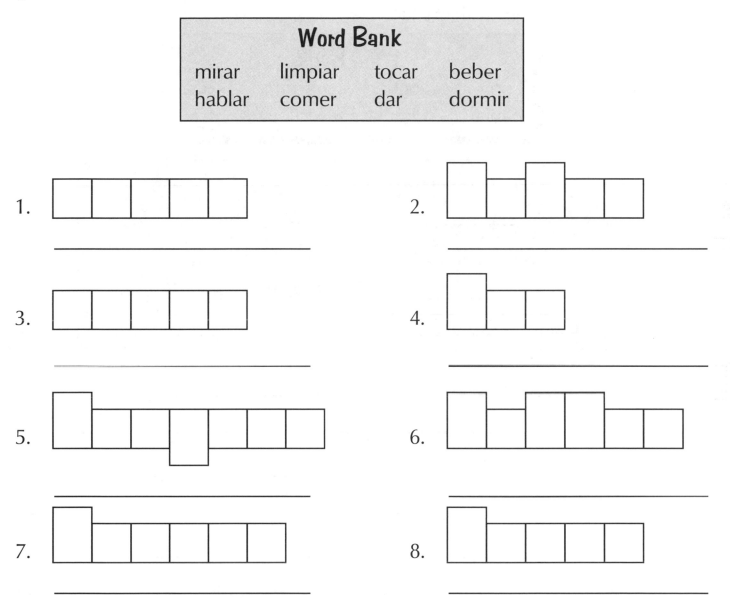

Word Bank

mirar	limpiar	tocar	beber
hablar	comer	dar	dormir

1.

2.

3.

4.

5.

6.

7.

8.

English

to eat	to look at	to speak	to touch
to clean	to sleep	to drink	to give

First Sentences

Create original sentences in Spanish using these sentence starters and the verbs in the Word Bank. You may use one sentence starter more than once. Write the English meanings on the lines below the Spanish.

Word Bank

comer	beber	dormir	tocar
hablar	limpiar	mirar	dar

Sentence Starters

Me gusta _____ .   (I like _____ .)

No me gusta _____ .   (I don't like _____ .)

Quiero _____ .   (I want _____ .)

Necesito _____ .   (I need _____ .)

1. _____

   _____

2. _____

   _____

3. _____

   _____

4. _____

   _____

5. _____

   _____

Nombre_____

Action Words

Refer to the Word Bank to write the Spanish word that matches each picture.

Word Bank	comer	estudiar	limpiar	mirar	jugar	dar
	hablar	beber	dormir	trabajar	tocar	ir

to clean

to touch

to eat

to speak — hablar

to watch

to drink

to give

to sleep

to study

to go

to work

to play

The Complete Book of Spanish

Reading and Writing

Circle the Spanish words that you find in the word search. Write the English meanings at the bottom of the page next to the Spanish words from the puzzle.

r	c	c	i	r	h	x	n	l	e	p	r
t	e	o	o	e	d	z	u	s	r	e	l
r	b	m	i	n	h	x	t	a	b	r	i
a	s	s	o	g	t	u	d	e	w	c	m
b	v	g	c	c	d	e	b	w	r	i	p
a	s	v	y	i	r	r	s	j	e	b	i
j	r	v	a	a	h	q	i	t	e	r	a
a	e	r	c	a	r	r	u	m	a	e	r
r	v	s	b	a	b	u	a	i	r	r	r
s	u	l	g	i	b	i	z	r	t	o	o
b	a	u	g	g	w	n	a	j	i	a	d
r	j	n	d	x	r	a	c	o	t	m	r

Spanish Word	English	Spanish Word	English
comer	_____	jugar	_____
hablar	_____	dormir	_____
estudiar	_____	mirar	_____
beber	_____	trabajar	_____
limpiar	_____	tocar	_____
ir	_____	dar	_____

Capitals

Spanish uses capital letters less often than the English language. Follow these rules as your guide.

Capitalization Rules

1. All Spanish sentences begin with capital letters.

2. Names of people begin with capital letters.

3. Names of places (cities, regions, countries, continents) and holidays begin with capital letters.

4. Titles are not capitalized unless abbreviated (*señor–Sr., usted–Ud.*).

5. Some words that are normally capitalized in English may not be capitalized in Spanish (nationalities, religions, languages, months, and days).

Write *sí* if the word should be capitalized. Write *no* if it should remain lowercase.

1. sarah _____

2. inglés _____

3. navidad _____

4. español _____

5. mexicano _____

6. áfrica _____

7. señor _____

8. enero _____

9. domingo _____

10. católico _____

11. santa fe _____

12. viernes _____

13. méxico _____

14. julio _____

15. colorado _____

16. miguel _____

The Complete Book of Spanish

Categories

Read the list of words given. Write the words in the proper columns. If the word needs a capital letter, write it that way.

los ángeles	españa	ustedes	americano	lunes
maría	susana	san antonio	américa del norte	méxico
uds.	sr.	santa fe	español	católico
inglés	sra.	océano pacífico	señora	señor
san diego	viernes	juan	josé	
señorita	cuba	septiembre	mexicano	

People	Places	Titles	Not Capitalized

Introductions and Greetings

¡Hola!

¿Cómo te llamas?

Me llamo...

The Complete Book of Spanish

Introductions and Greetings

¿Cómo estás?

bien

así, así

¡Adiós!

mal

Introductions and Greetings

Say the Spanish introductions and greetings out loud.

¡Hola!

Hello

¿Cómo te llamas?

What is your name?

Me llamo...

My name is...

¿Cómo estás?..

How are you?

bien

mal

así, así

¡Adiós!

Good-bye

The Complete Book of Spanish

Pictures of Greetings

Say the greeting out loud. Circle the picture that tells the meaning of each word.

The Complete Book of Spanish

Nombre _____

Greetings Paste Up

Cut out a picture from a magazine that shows the meaning of each greeting and glue it next to the correct word or words.

¡Hola!

¿Cómo te llamas?

Me llamo...

¿Cómo estás?

bien

mal

así, así

¡Adiós!

The Complete Book of Spanish

Polite Words

Say each Spanish expression out loud.

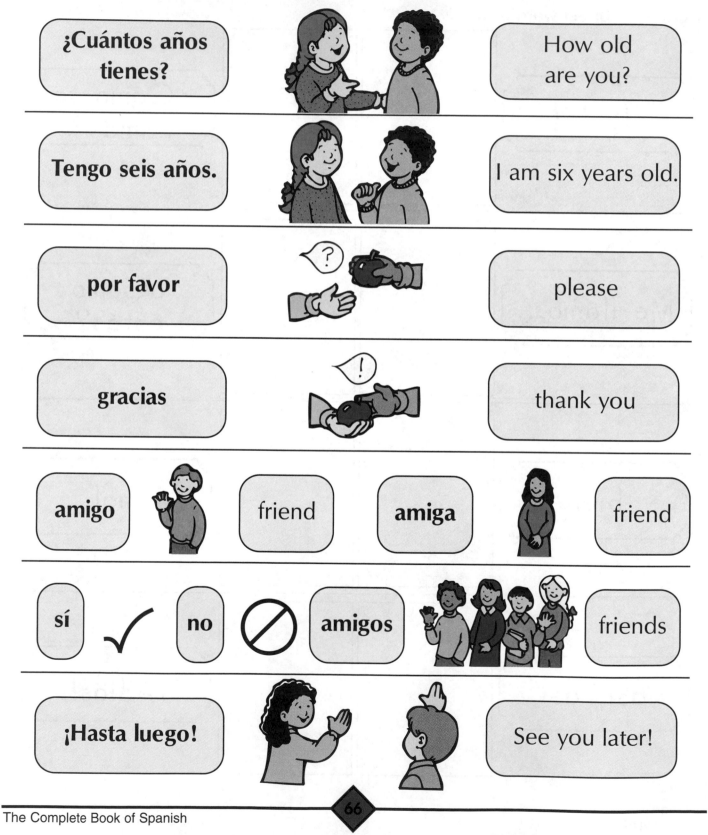

¿Cuántos años tienes?	How old are you?
Tengo seis años.	I am six years old.
por favor	please
gracias	thank you

amigo — friend   amiga — friend

sí ✓   no ⊘   amigos — friends

¡Hasta luego! — See you later!

Introductions Review

Say each expression out loud. Circle the picture that tells the meaning of each word.

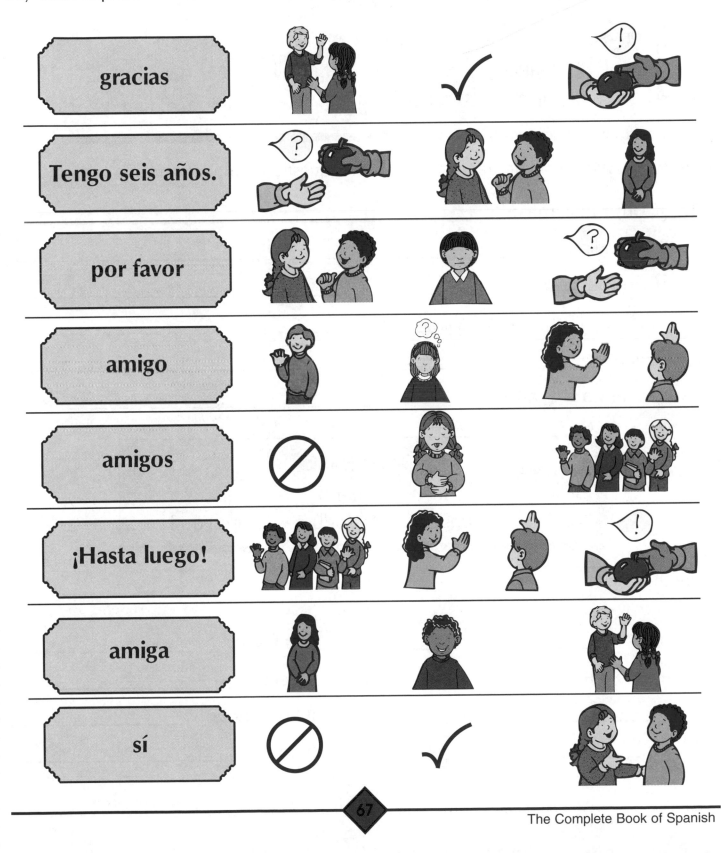

The Complete Book of Spanish

What's Your Name?

Word Bank

I'm so-so.	What's your name?	I'm well/fine.
I'm ____ years old.	I'm not doing well.	My name is ___.
I'm not well.	How are you?	How old are you?

Refer to the Word Bank to translate the Spanish questions and answers into English.

1. ¿Cómo te llamas? _____

    Me llamo _____. _____

2. ¿Cómo estás? _____

    Estoy bien/mal/así así. _____

3. ¿Cuántos años tienes? _____

    Tengo ___ años. _____

Word Bank

hello	please	friend	yes
no	thank you	goodbye	See you later!

Write the English meaning after the Spanish word.

4. hola _____

5. amigo, amiga _____

6. sí _____

7. no _____

8. por favor _____

9. gracias _____

10. ¡Hasta luego! _____

11. adiós _____

Word Blocks

Write the Spanish words from the Word Bank that fit in these word blocks. Don't forget the punctuation. Write the English meanings below the blocks.

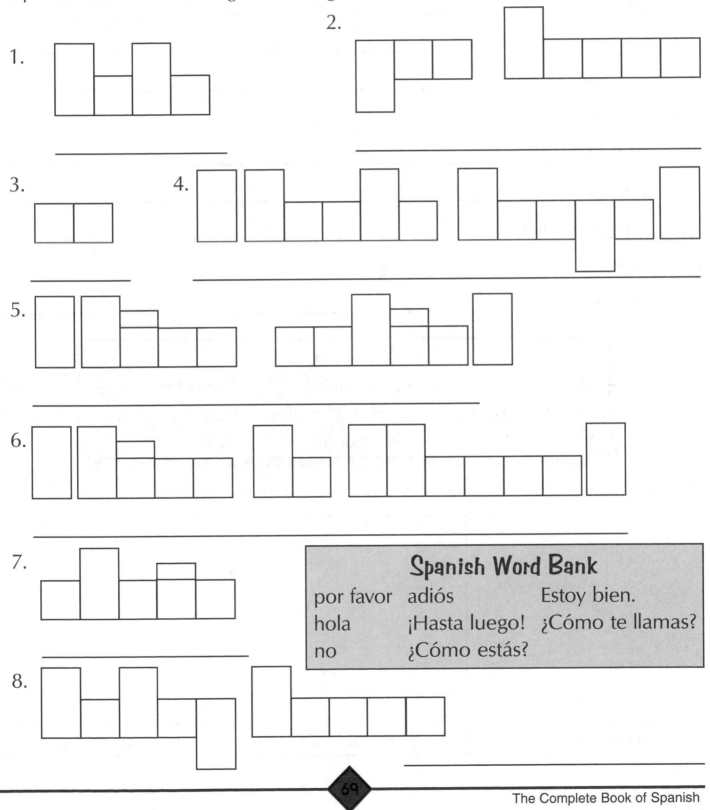

1.

2.

3.

4.

5.

6.

7.

8.

Spanish Word Bank

por favor	adiós	Estoy bien.
hola	¡Hasta luego!	¿Cómo te llamas?
no	¿Cómo estás?	

The Complete Book of Spanish

Greetings

Write the English meaning of the Spanish words and phrases.

1. señor   _____

2. señora   _____

3. señorita   _____

4. maestro   _____

5. maestra   _____

6. ¡Buenos días! _____

7. ¡Buenas tardes! _____

8. ¡Buenas noches! _____

9. Vamos a contar. _____

Word Bank

Mr.	Good night!	Good morning!
Good afternoon!	teacher (female)	teacher (male)
Miss	Let's count.	Mrs.

Draw a picture to show the time of day that you use each expression.

¡Buenos días!	¡Buenas tardes!	¡Buenas noches!

Spanish Greetings

Write the Spanish word for each clue in the crossword puzzle.

Across

1. bad
4. good
7. teacher (male)
9. friend (female)
10. Mr.
11. Miss

Word Bank

amiga	mal
señora	señor
maestra	bien
adiós	hola
señorita	gracias
amigo	maestro

Down

2. friend (male)
3. hello
5. thank you
6. goodbye
7. teacher (female)
8. Mrs.

The Complete Book of Spanish

Greetings

Refer to the Word Bank to translate the Spanish greetings, questions, and answers.

¡Buenos días! _____

¡Buenas tardes! _____

¡Buenas noches! _____

¿Cómo estás? _____

    bien, gracias _____

    mal   _____

    así así   _____

¿Cómo te llamas? _____

    Me llamo _____ . _____

¿Cuántos años tienes? _____

    Tengo _____ años. _____

adiós _____ hola _____

Word Bank

goodbye
Good morning!
I am _____ years old.
fine, thank you
Good afternoon!
hello
How old are you?
How are you?
What is your name?
My name is _____ .
not well
ok/so-so
Good night!

Word Bank

teacher (m/f)	Miss	no
Mr.	friend (m/f)	please
Mrs.	yes	

Refer to the Word Bank to translate the Spanish vocabulary.

amigo/amiga _____

sí _____ no _____ por favor _____

señor _____ señora _____

maestro/maestra _____

señorita _____

Find the Words

Circle the Spanish words that you find in the word search. Write the English meanings at the bottom of the page next to the Spanish words from the puzzle.

y	q	d	t	h	s	a	s	s	n	m	m
o	w	m	o	r	m	e	e	x	o	a	a
m	o	l	o	i	n	n	h	k	n	e	e
u	a	n	g	o	o	m	p	k	k	s	s
q	e	a	r	r	u	g	l	o	l	t	t
s	s	i	a	b	m	w	h	z	e	r	r
s	t	a	a	m	n	v	e	m	o	a	
a	w	i	d	m	x	i	i	j	d	j	
x	b	o	l	c	i	i	n	s	i	x	x
w	t	q	f	v	a	o	g	e	l	t	u
t	o	n	m	s	h	r	s	o	i	a	k
m	g	b	f	n	f	z	g	w	u	b	m

Spanish Word	English	Spanish Word	English
amigo	_____	adiós	_____
gracias	_____	maestro	_____
mal	_____	señor	_____
amiga	_____	bien	_____
hola	_____	maestra	_____
no	_____	señora	_____
señorita	_____	sí	_____

73

Nombre_____

Days

lunes miércoles viernes domingo

martes jueves sábado

Monday	Tuesday	Wednesday	Thursday	Friday	Saturday	Sunday
		1	2	3	4	5
6	7	8	9	10	11	12
13	14	15	16	17	18	19
20	21	22	23	24	25	26
27	28	29	30			

The Complete Book of Spanish

Nombre_____

Months

enero	febrero	marzo

abril	mayo	junio

julio	agosto	septiembre

octubre	noviembre	diciembre

The Complete Book of Spanish

Nombre_____

Seven Days

Copy the Spanish words for the days of the week. In Spanish-speaking countries, *lunes* is the first day of the week.

Monday	**lunes**	_____
Tuesday	**martes**	_____
Wednesday	**miércoles**	_____
Thursday	**jueves**	_____
Friday	**viernes**	_____
Saturday	**sábado**	_____
Sunday	**domingo**	_____

Draw a line to match the Spanish and English days of the week.

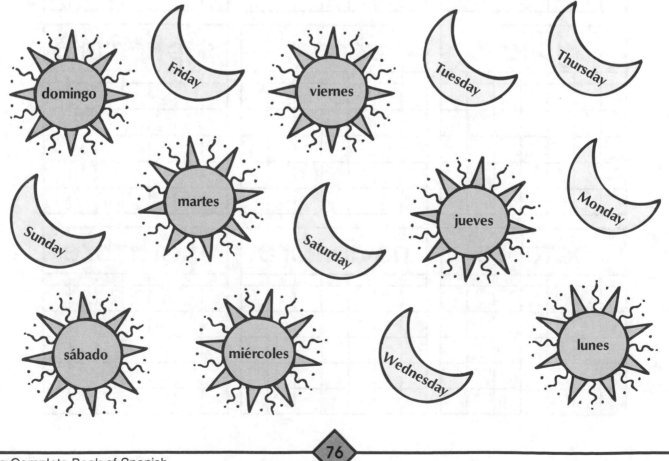

Nombre_____

Puzzle of the Week

Write the Spanish words in the puzzle.

Across

2. Thursday
7. Wednesday

Down

1. Monday
3. Saturday
4. Friday
5. Sunday
6. Tuesday

Word Bank

jueves   domingo   martes
sábado   viernes   lunes
            miércoles

The Complete Book of Spanish

Nombre_____

Calendar Game

On your turn roll the die, move your marker, and say the number and day of the week in Spanish.

• If you can't remember a Spanish word, ask for help and skip a turn.

• The winner is the player who first translates a date from the bottom row.

• For two to four players.

Monday	Tuesday	Wednesday	Thursday	Friday	Saturday	Sunday
	start	1	2	3	4	5
6	7	8	9	10	11	12
13	14	15	16	17	18	19
20	21	22	23	24	25	26
27	28	29	30			
finish line						

Yesterday and Today

Write the Spanish words for the days of the week. Remember, in Spanish-speaking countries, Monday is the first day of the week.

Word Bank

miércoles   jueves   sábado
viernes   lunes   martes
domingo

Monday   _____

Tuesday   _____

Wednesday   _____

Thursday   _____

Friday   _____

Saturday   _____

Sunday   _____

If today is Monday, yesterday was Sunday. Complete the following chart by identifying the missing days in Spanish. The first one is done for you.

ayer (yesterday)	hoy (today)	mañana (tomorrow)
martes	miércoles	jueves
lunes		
		sábado
	domingo	
	jueves	
		martes
viernes		

Do It Tomorrow

Circle the Spanish words you find in the word search. Write the English meanings at the bottom of the page next to the Spanish words from the puzzle.

a	a	m	e	o	k	o	i	s	s	s	x
j	y	j	k	j	s	j	e	e	f	á	i
q	x	e	c	x	h	l	n	x	u	b	b
r	d	v	r	w	o	u	l	u	h	a	t
x	y	g	i	c	l	m	p	u	h	d	w
f	j	e	r	e	o	b	j	u	v	o	a
q	y	é	h	f	r	g	x	c	k	l	n
p	i	o	j	a	d	n	n	k	z	j	a
m	y	z	s	f	l	h	e	i	c	f	ñ
b	o	n	q	b	w	a	d	s	m	i	a
m	a	r	t	e	s	z	s	n	z	o	m
j	u	e	v	e	s	b	o	o	m	h	d

Spanish Word	English	Spanish Word	English
jueves	_____	domingo	_____
viernes	_____	hoy	_____
ayer	_____	miércoles	_____
lunes	_____	martes	_____
mañana	_____	sábado	_____

Rain in April

Refer to the Word Bank to write the Spanish word for the given month. Then, in the box, draw a picture of something that happens in that month of the year. Remember that Spanish months do not begin with capital letters.

Word Bank

agosto	septiembre	noviembre	mayo
junio	enero	octubre	febrero
marzo	julio	diciembre	abril

January _____		July _____	
February _____		August _____	
March _____		September _____	
April _____		October _____	
May _____		November _____	
June _____		December _____	

Nombre_____

Writing Practice

Copy the following paragraph in your best handwriting. Practice reading it out loud.

Hay doce meses en un año. Diciembre, enero y febrero son en el invierno. Marzo, abril y mayo son en la primavera. Junio, julio y agosto son en el verano. Septiembre, octubre y noviembre son en el otoño. ¿Cuál es tú favorito mes del año?

The Complete Book of Spanish

Spanish Months

Write the Spanish word for the clue words in the crossword puzzle.

Across

4. July
9. May
10. September
11. June
12. January

Down

1. April
2. November
3. December
5. March
6. February
7. August
8. October

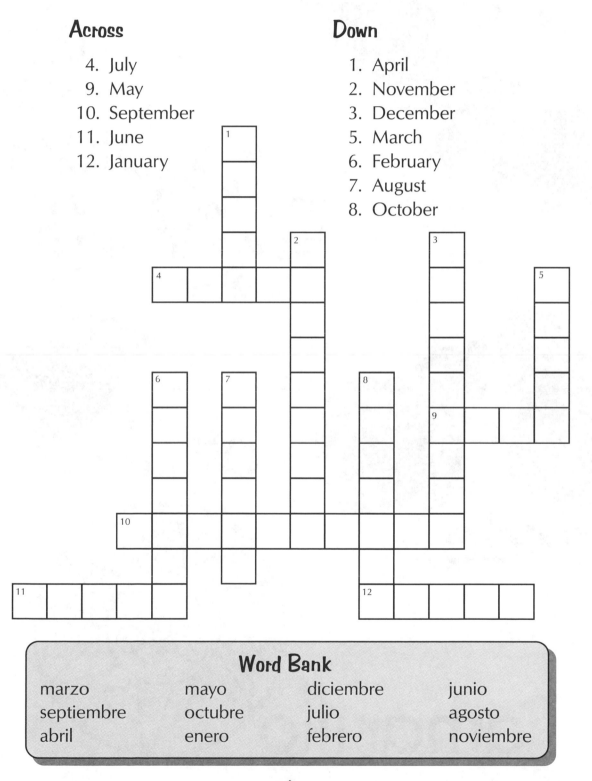

Word Bank

marzo	mayo	diciembre	junio
septiembre	octubre	julio	agosto
abril	enero	febrero	noviembre

The Complete Book of Spanish

Colors

negro

blanco

verde

azul

amarillo

Colors

café

anaranjado

morado

rojo

rosado

Color Introduction

Say the words out loud. Color the word with the correct color.

The Complete Book of Spanish

Nombre_____

Pictures to Color

Color the pictures according to each color word.

rojo

azul

verde

anaranjado

morado

amarillo

The Complete Book of Spanish

Rainbow Colors

Color the picture according to the color words shown.

The Complete Book of Spanish

Color the Cars

Color the cars according to the color words shown.

Birds of Color

Color the birds according to the words listed.

The Complete Book of Spanish

Nombre_____

House of Colors

Color each crayon with the correct color for the Spanish word. Add something with your favorite color.

☐ rojo   ☐ negro   ☐ café   ☐ rosado
☐ azul   ☐ amarillo   ☐ blanco   ☐ verde

The Complete Book of Spanish

Color the Flowers

Color each flower with the correct color for the Spanish word.

- ☐ azul
- ☐ verde
- ☐ café
- ☐ rojo
- ☐ amarillo
- ☐ morado
- ☐ rosado
- ☐ anaranjado

The Complete Book of Spanish

Nombre_____

Color Search

Cut out pictures from a magazine that match the colors below. Glue each picture next to the correct color word.

rojo		amarillo	
azul		café	
verde		negro	
anaranjado		blanco	
morado		rosado	

The Complete Book of Spanish

Moving Colors

Color the pictures according to the words listed.

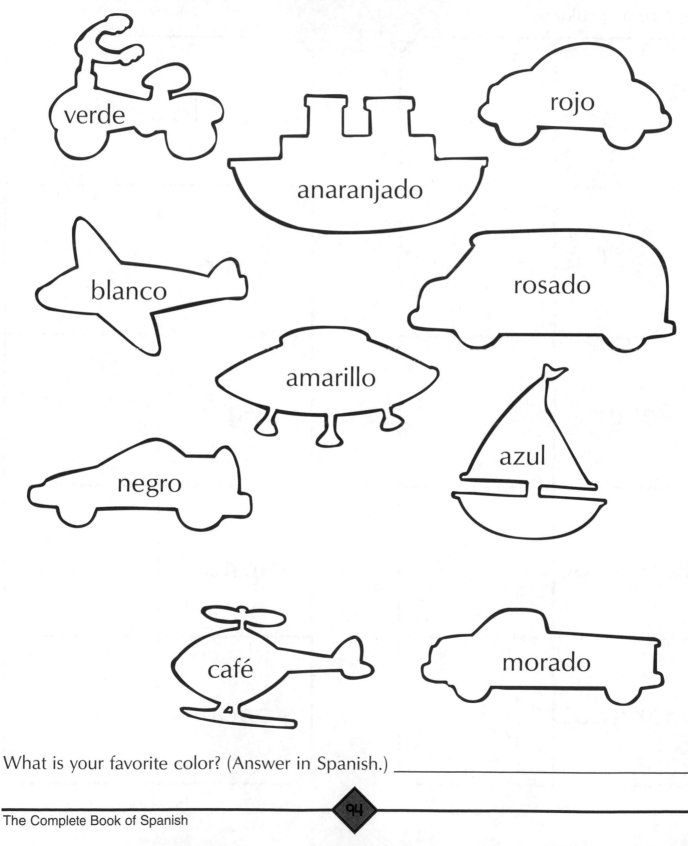

verde

anaranjado

rojo

blanco

rosado

amarillo

negro

azul

café

morado

What is your favorite color? (Answer in Spanish.) _____

Color Away

Write the English word below the Spanish color listed. Use the words at the bottom to help you. Color the pictures using that color.

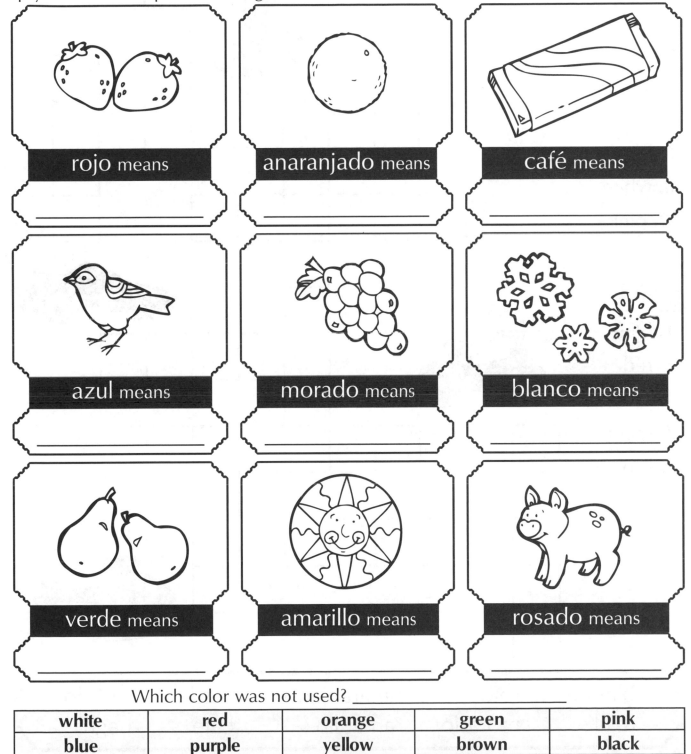

rojo means

_____

anaranjado means

_____

café means

_____

azul means

_____

morado means

_____

blanco means

_____

verde means

_____

amarillo means

_____

rosado means

_____

Which color was not used? _____

white	red	orange	green	pink
blue	purple	yellow	brown	black

Color Crossword

Write the correct Spanish color words in the spaces.
Follow the English color clues.

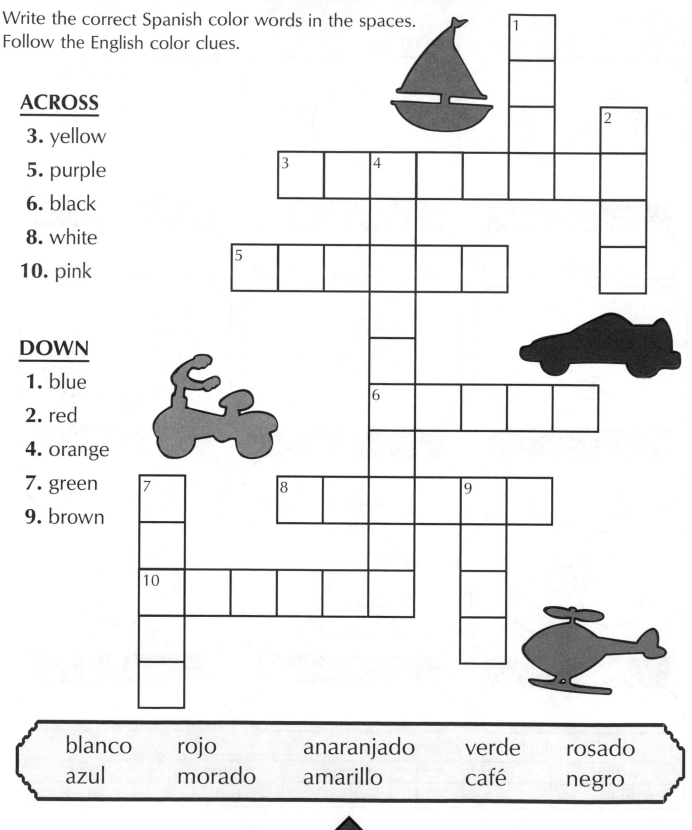

ACROSS

3. yellow

5. purple

6. black

8. white

10. pink

DOWN

1. blue

2. red

4. orange

7. green

9. brown

blanco　　rojo　　anaranjado　　verde　　rosado
azul　　morado　　amarillo　　café　　negro

Nombre_____

Color Copy

Copy the following words in the color of each word.
Which word is hard to see with the actual color? _____

rojo

azul

verde

anaranjado

morado

amarillo

café

negro

blanco

rosado

The Complete Book of Spanish

Colorful Flowers

Color the flowers according to the Spanish color words shown below.

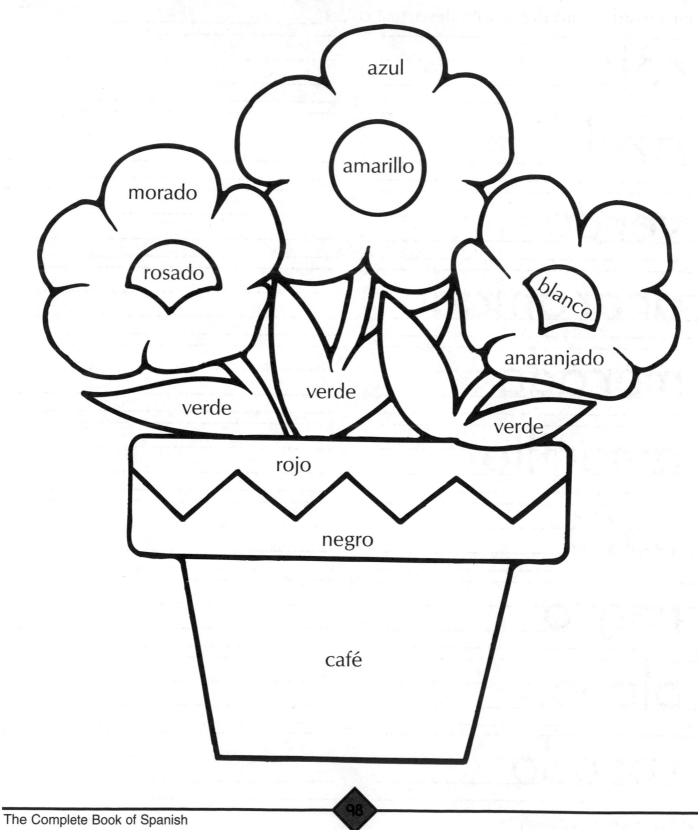

azul

amarillo

morado

rosado

blanco

anaranjado

verde

verde

verde

rojo

negro

café

Nombre_____

Color Find

Circle the Spanish color words that you find in the wordsearch. Then, write the English meaning of each word.

é	o	a	p	v	o	r	n	u	a	j	v
f	c	x	z	q	d	b	i	a	r	e	a
a	n	n	a	u	i	g	y	i	r	n	n
c	a	c	a	m	l	c	j	d	a	j	y
r	l	o	t	l	a	i	e	r	z	o	r
o	b	g	r	d	b	r	a	t	f	g	l
l	q	d	b	v	o	n	i	s	b	b	f
o	v	s	d	d	j	h	n	l	u	f	o
c	m	y	a	a	o	k	x	e	l	t	j
e	t	r	d	i	o	c	n	k	g	o	o
d	o	o	p	w	q	s	i	d	x	r	r
m	r	o	s	a	d	o	q	k	k	t	o

Spanish Word	English	Spanish Word	English
blanco	_____	amarillo	_____
azul	_____	verde	_____
rojo	_____	café	_____
morado	_____	rosado	_____
anaranjado	_____	negro	_____

The Complete Book of Spanish

Draw and Color

In each box, write the Spanish color word. Use the Word Bank below to help you. Then, draw and color a picture of something that is usually that color.

red is _____	orange is _____	brown is _____
blue is _____	purple is _____	black is _____
green is _____	yellow is _____	pink is _____

Which Spanish color from the Word Bank is not used above? _____

Word Bank

blanco	rojo	amarillo	rosado
azul	morado	verde	negro
	anaranjado	café	

Butterfly Garden

Color the butterfly garden as indicated in Spanish.

Across the Spectrum

Write the Spanish for each clue word in the crossword puzzle.

Across

2. blue
4. brown
6. red
7. purple
8. white
9. black

Down

1. green
2. yellow
3. pink
5. orange

Food

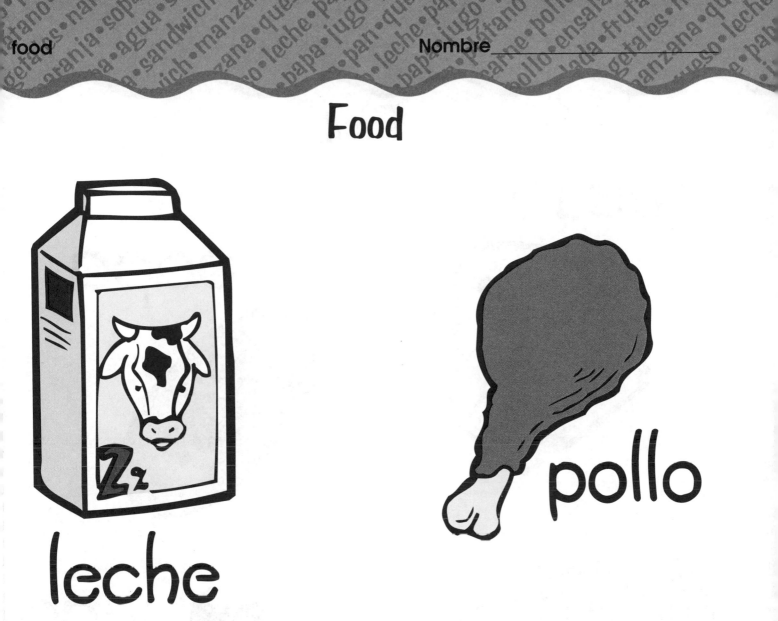

leche

pollo

ensalada

Nombre_____

Food

queso

papa

pan

jugo

Food and Drink

Say the Spanish words for some delicious foods and drinks out loud.

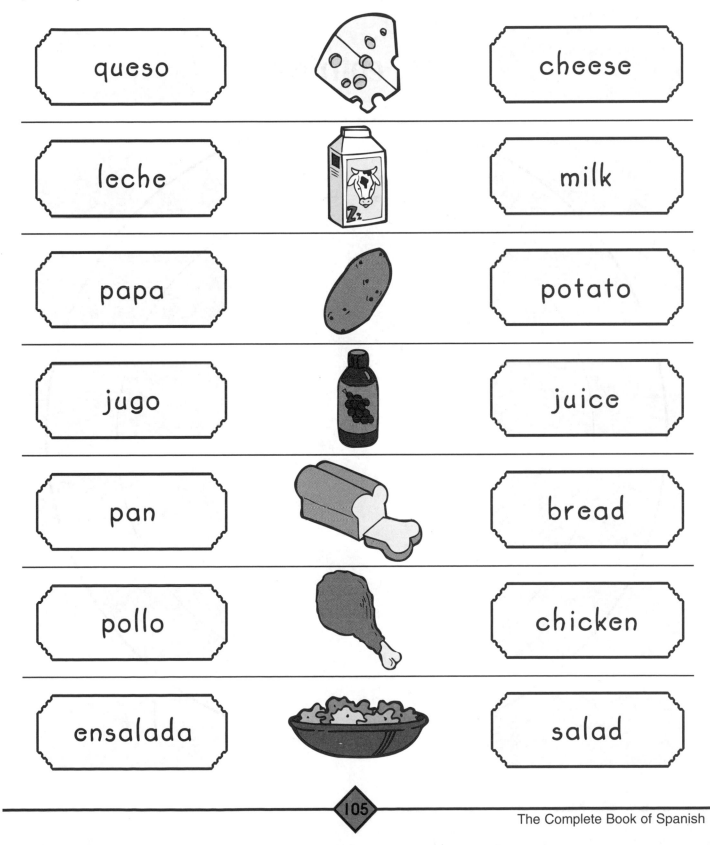

queso		cheese
leche		milk
papa		potato
jugo		juice
pan		bread
pollo		chicken
ensalada		salad

My Meal

Draw or cut out pictures of food and glue them on the plate to make a meal. Which food is your favorite?

Mi comida

Nombre_____

Food Meanings

Say each word out loud. Circle the picture that shows the meaning of each word.

papa

ensalada

queso

pan

leche

pollo

jugo

The Complete Book of Spanish

Mixed-Up Food

Draw a line from the word to the food picture.

papa

ensalada

queso

pan

leche

jugo

pollo

Food Words

Say each word out loud. Write the English word next to it.

queso

_____

leche

_____

papa

_____

jugo

pan

_____

pollo

_____

ensalada _____

Color the blocks with letters.
Do not color the blocks with numbers. What word did you find? _____

7	x	7	7	7	7	7	7	7	7	7	x	7	7	7	7	7	7	7
7	x	7	7	7	7	7	7	7	7	7	x	7	7	7	7	7	7	7
7	x	7	7	7	7	7	7	7	7	7	x	7	7	7	7	7	7	7
7	x	7	x	x	x	7	x	x	x	7	x	7	7	7	x	x	x	7
7	x	7	x	7	x	7	x	7	7	7	x	x	x	7	x	7	x	7
7	x	7	x	x	x	7	x	7	7	7	x	7	x	7	x	x	x	7
7	x	7	x	7	7	7	x	7	7	7	x	7	x	7	x	7	7	7
7	x	7	x	x	x	7	x	x	x	7	x	7	x	7	x	x	x	7

109

Nombre _____

Food Riddles

Answer the riddles. Use the size and shape of the word blocks along with the answers at the bottom to help you.

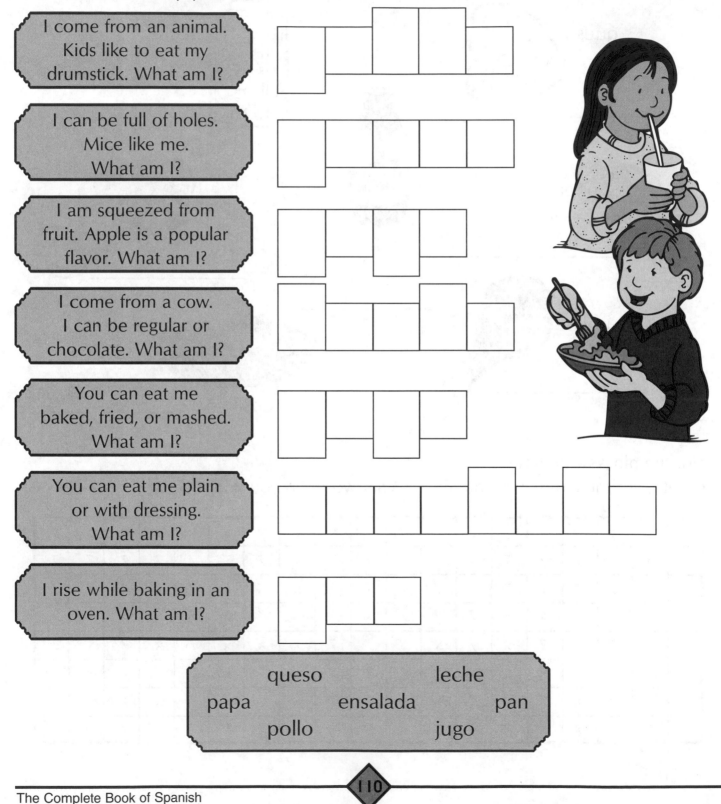

I come from an animal. Kids like to eat my drumstick. What am I?

I can be full of holes. Mice like me. What am I?

I am squeezed from fruit. Apple is a popular flavor. What am I?

I come from a cow. I can be regular or chocolate. What am I?

You can eat me baked, fried, or mashed. What am I?

You can eat me plain or with dressing. What am I?

I rise while baking in an oven. What am I?

queso   leche

papa   ensalada   pan

pollo   jugo

New Food Words

Say each word out loud. Copy each word and color the picture.

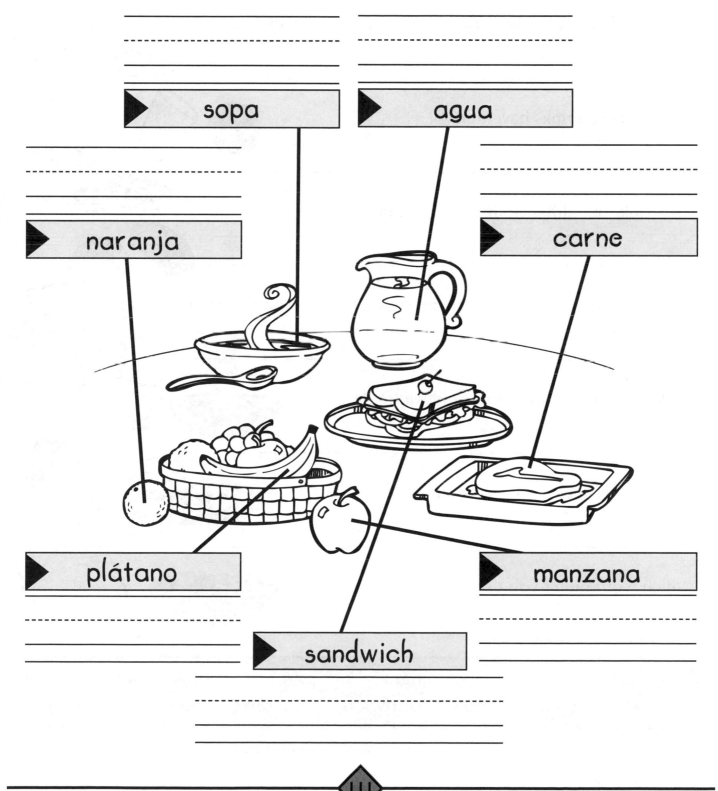

▶ sopa

▶ agua

▶ naranja

▶ carne

▶ plátano

▶ manzana

▶ sandwich

Nombre_____

Use the Clues

Use the clues and the Word Bank at the bottom of the page to find the answers.
Do not use any answer more than once.

1. You would not eat either of these fruits until you peel them.

_____   _____

2. Both of these drinks have a flavor.

_____   _____

3. You could put either of these on a sandwich.

_____   _____

4. These can be baked before eating. They all begin with the letter "p."

_____   _____   _____

5. These two go together on a cold winter day.

_____   _____

6. You use this liquid to wash this fruit.

_____   _____

7. Which word didn't you use?

_____

| queso | leche | papa | jugo | pan | pollo | ensalada |
| naranja | sopa | agua | sandwich | manzana | carne | plátano |

Check off each word as you use it.

The Complete Book of Spanish

Nombre_____

A Square Meal

Refer to the Word Bank to write the name of each food in Spanish.

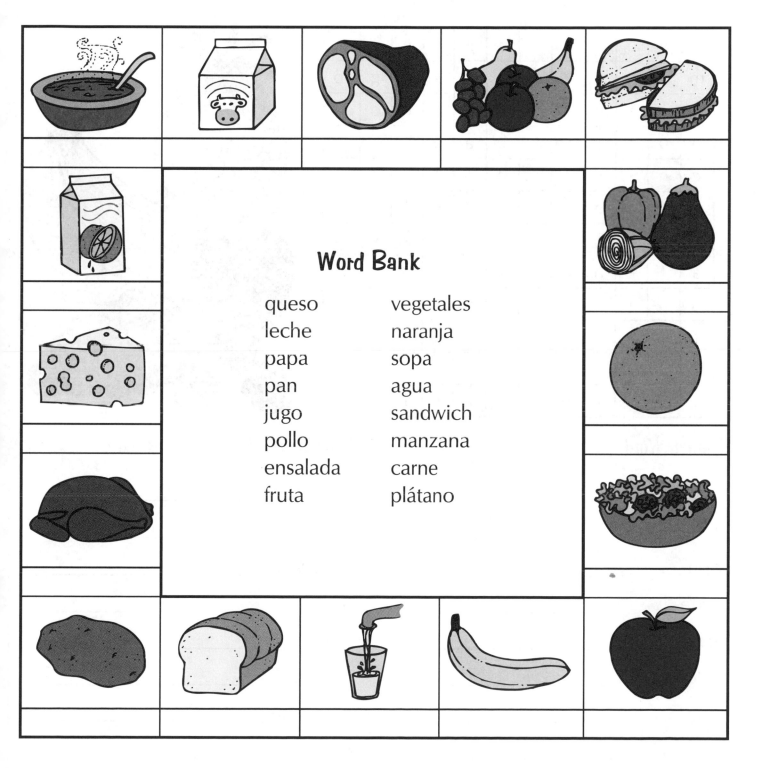

Word Bank

queso	vegetales
leche	naranja
papa	sopa
pan	agua
jugo	sandwich
pollo	manzana
ensalada	carne
fruta	plátano

Searching for Food

Circle the Spanish words that you find in the wordsearch. Then, write the English meaning of each word.

i	v	a	d	a	l	a	s	n	e	p	a
m	a	n	z	a	n	a	s	s	a	g	p
c	a	j	n	a	r	a	n	p	u	o	e
e	o	f	j	v	h	e	a	a	l	a	s
c	h	s	y	i	x	b	b	l	t	e	p
l	a	c	e	w	y	b	o	u	l	t	l
p	e	r	i	u	m	q	r	a	a	v	á
a	t	c	n	w	q	f	t	m	d	a	t
n	u	i	h	e	d	e	o	s	x	p	a
r	m	r	t	e	g	n	i	g	l	o	n
f	r	s	k	e	j	o	a	w	u	s	o
i	r	a	v	p	a	h	h	s	i	j	v

Spanish Word　　**English**

queso　_____

jugo　_____

sopa　_____

carne　_____

leche　_____

pollo　_____

agua　_____

plátano　_____

Spanish Word　　**English**

papa　_____

ensalada　_____

sandwich　_____

fruta　_____

pan　_____

naranja　_____

manzana　_____

vegetales　_____

Food Groups

Write the Spanish food words to match the pictures.

Word Bank

ensalada	pan	sopa	sandwich
plátano	naranja	fruta	leche
manzana	queso	jugo	agua
papa	carne	vegetales	pollo

cheese	meat	soup	orange
juice	vegetables	water	bread
potato	salad	chicken	banana
fruit	apple	sandwich	milk

The Complete Book of Spanish

Nombre_____

Eat It Up

Write the Spanish for the clue words in the crossword puzzle.

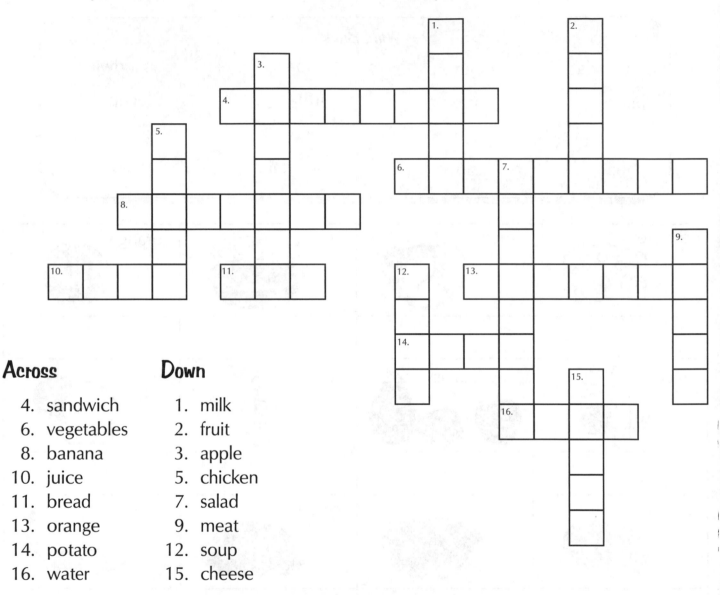

Across

4. sandwich
6. vegetables
8. banana
10. juice
11. bread
13. orange
14. potato
16. water

Down

1. milk
2. fruit
3. apple
5. chicken
7. salad
9. meat
12. soup
15. cheese

Word Bank

ensalada	plátano	manzana	papa
pan	naranja	fruta	queso
carne	sopa	jugo	vegetales
sandwich	leche	agua	pollo

Animals

perro

pájaro

rana

pez

vaca

Animals

abeja

pato

gato

oso

caballo

Nombre_____

Animals All Around

Copy each word and color the pictures.

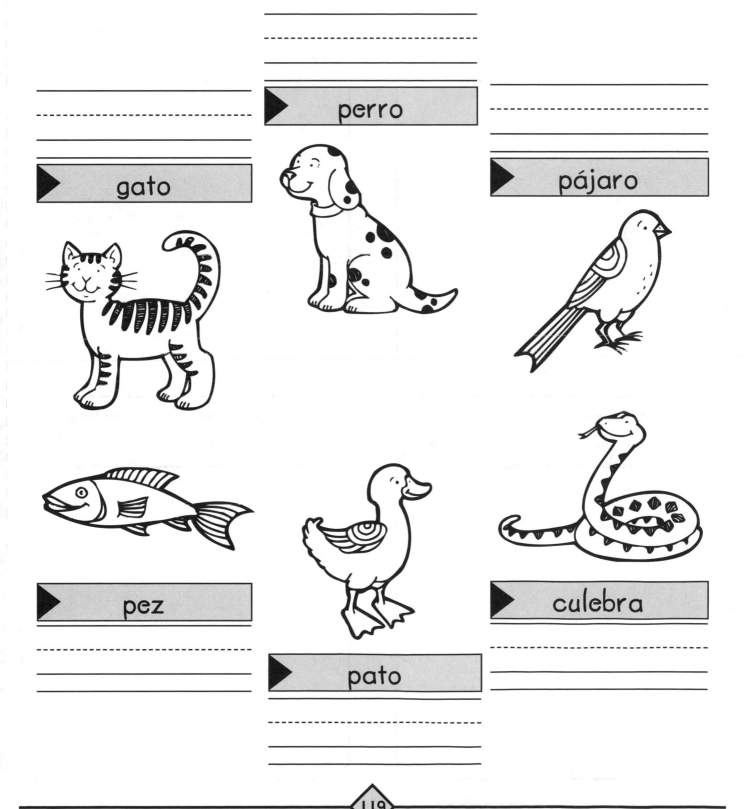

perro

gato

pájaro

pez

pato

culebra

The Complete Book of Spanish

Nombre_____

Animal Art

Choose four animals and draw each animal in its home. Label it with the Spanish animal word.

Animal Crossword

Use the picture clues to complete the puzzle. Choose from the Spanish words at the bottom of the page. One is done for you.

| gato | perro | pájaro |
| pez | pato | culebra |

The Complete Book of Spanish

Use the Clues

Answer the questions. Use the clues and the Spanish words at the bottom of the page. You may use answers more than once.

1. Both words begin with the same letter, and both animals have feathers.

_____   _____

2. These two animals walk and are house pets.

_____   _____

3. Both animals begin with the same letter. One quacks and the other barks.

_____   _____

4. Both of these animals like to live in the water.

_____   _____

5. These animals do not have fur or feathers.

_____   _____

6. The first animal likes to chase and catch the second animal. They both end with the letter *o*.

_____   _____

gato	perro	pájaro
pez	pato	culebra

Nombre_____

Pet Parade

In each box, copy the name of each animal in Spanish. Write the Spanish words next to the English words at the bottom of the page.

pájaro	bird	caballo	horse
perro	dog	oso	bear
rana	frog	gato	cat
vaca	cow	pato	duck
abeja	bee	pez	fish

Write the Spanish words from above next to the English words.

cat _____   cow _____   duck _____

dog _____   horse _____   frog _____

bird _____   bear _____   bee _____

fish _____

The Complete Book of Spanish

Three Little Kittens

Draw a picture to match the Spanish phrase in each box.

seis pájaros	cuatro perros
nueve abejas	siete osos
tres gatos	dos vacas
cinco patos	ocho caballos
diez ranas	un pez

Name That Animal

On your turn roll the die, move your marker, and say the animal name in Spanish.

• If you can't remember a Spanish word, ask for help and skip a turn.

• The winner is the player to reach the finish first.

• For two to four players.

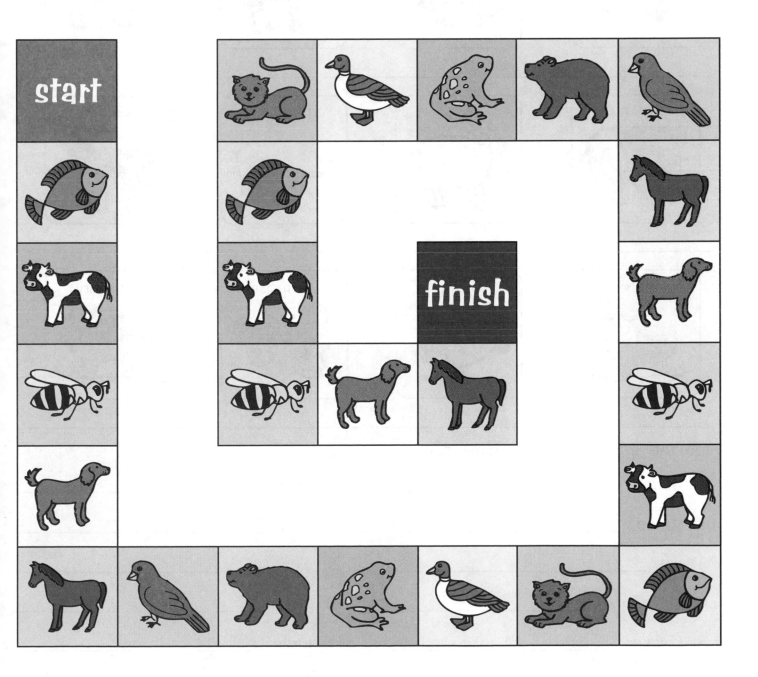

The Complete Book of Spanish

Nombre_____

Animal Match

Copy the Spanish word under each picture.

oso	rana	caballo	vaca

_____   _____   _____   _____

elefante	oveja	puerco	gallina

gato	tortuga	mariposa	dinosaurio

_____   _____   _____   _____

Write the Spanish for each animal name.

1. butterfly _____

2. sheep _____

3. cat _____

4. dinosaur _____

5. chicken _____

6. pig _____

7. cow _____

8. bear _____

9. elephant _____

10. horse _____

11. turtle _____

12. frog _____

Rainbow Roundup

Copy the following Spanish sentences on the lines provided. Then, write the English meanings.

1. El oso es blanco. _____

_____

2. El puerco es rosado. _____

_____

3. La rana es roja. _____

_____

4. La tortuga es verde. _____

_____

5. El dinosaurio es azul. _____

_____

6. El gato es anaranjado. _____

_____

7. La gallina es amarilla. _____

_____

8. El caballo es café. _____

_____

9. La mariposa es morada. _____

_____

Clothing

vestido

gorro

camisa

Clothing

calcetines

zapatos

pantalones

Clothing

Say each word out loud.

camisa		shirt
pantalones		pants
vestido		dress
calcetines		socks
zapatos		shoes
gorro		cap

Clothing Match-Ups

Draw a line from the word to match the correct picture. Color the picture.

camisa

pantalones

zapatos

gorro

vestido

calcetines

The Complete Book of Spanish

How Are You?

Draw or cut out pictures of clothes to make a boy or girl. Write the names of the clothes next to them in Spanish.

The Complete Book of Spanish

Nombre_____

Clothes to Color

Cut out pictures and glue them next to the correct words.

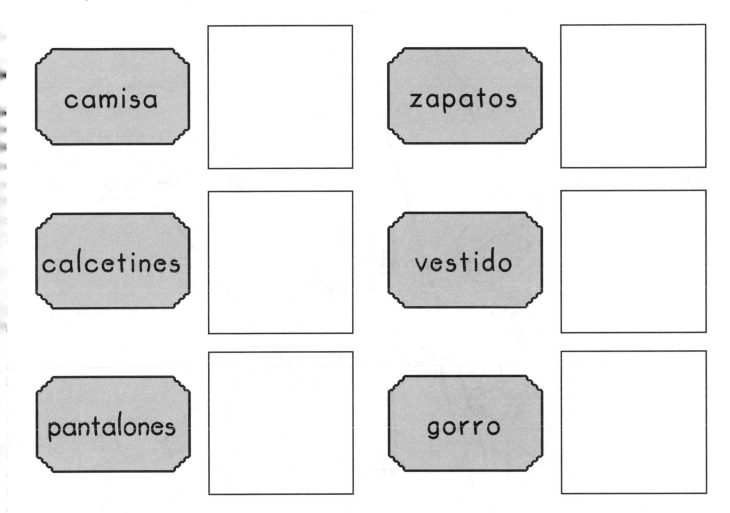

camisa

zapatos

calcetines

vestido

pantalones

gorro

Try this: Color each block with a letter X inside. Do not color the blocks with numbers. What hidden word did you find? _____

8	8	8	8	8	8	8	8	8	8	8	8	8	8	8	8	8	8	8	8	8	8
8	8	x	x	x	8	x	x	x	8	x	x	x	8	x	x	x	8	x	x	x	8
8	8	x	8	x	8	x	8	x	8	x	8	x	8	x	8	x	8	x	8	x	8
8	8	x	x	x	8	x	8	x	8	x	8	8	x	8	8	8	x	8	x	8
8	8	8	8	x	8	x	x	x	8	x	8	8	8	x	8	8	8	x	x	x	8
8	8	x	8	x	8	8	8	8	8	8	8	8	8	8	8	8	8	8	8	8	8
8	8	x	x	x	8	8	8	8	8	8	8	8	8	8	8	8	8	8	8	8	8

The Complete Book of Spanish

Clothing

Say each word out loud. Copy each word and color the picture.

pantalones

gorro

vestido

camisa

zapatos

calcetines

The Complete Book of Spanish

Nombre_____

Clothing

Say each word out loud. Copy each word and color the picture.

abrigo

chaqueta

falda

guantes

pantalones cortos

botas

The Complete Book of Spanish

Nombre_____

Remember These?

Fill in the blanks with the missing letters. Use the Spanish clothing words at the bottom to help you.

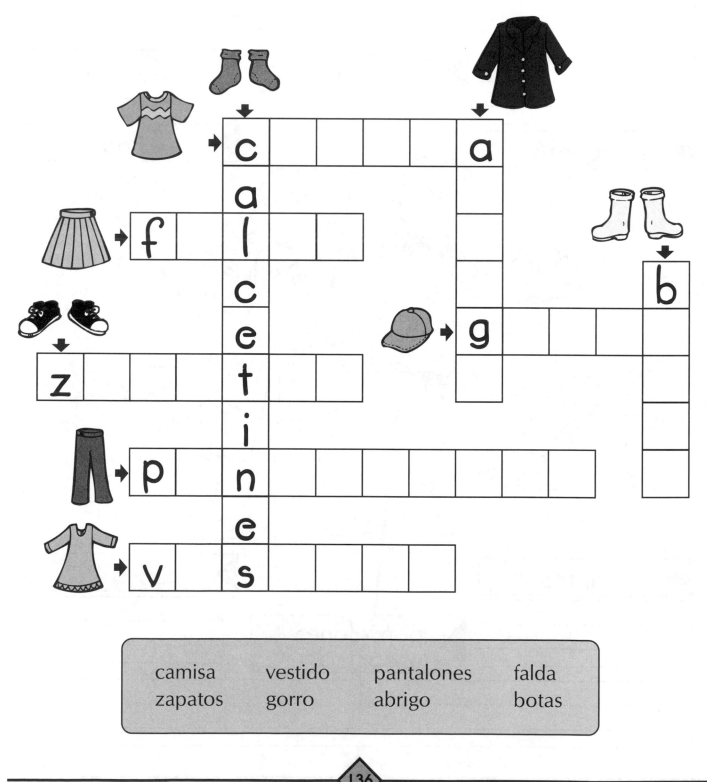

| camisa | vestido | pantalones | falda |
| zapatos | gorro | abrigo | botas |

The Complete Book of Spanish

What Belongs?

Circle the item that does not belong with the other two. Write the name in Spanish below its picture.

Circle the two items that are alike. Say the item in Spanish that is not like the other two. Color the pictures.

Clothes Closet

Refer to the Word Bank and write the Spanish word for each item of clothing pictured.

Word Bank			
vestido	calcetines	botas	zapatos
sombrero	cinturón	falda	chaqueta
guantes	pantalones cortos	pantalones	camisa

shirt		pants	
shorts		hat	
socks		skirt	
shoes		belt	
boots		dress	
gloves		jacket	

Nombre_____

Dressing Up

Write the Spanish word for each clue in the crossword puzzle.

Across

1. shoes
4. socks
7. dress
8. gloves
9. hat
10. shirt

Word Bank

cinturón	botas	camisa
guantes	calcetines	sombrero
chaqueta	falda	zapatos
pantalones	vestido	

Down

2. pants
3. skirt
4. jacket
5. belt
6. boots

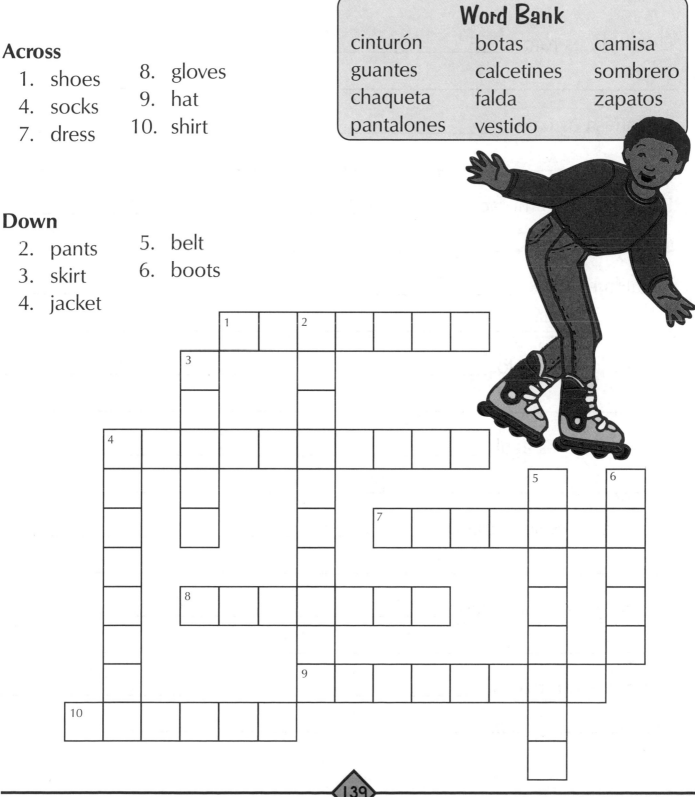

The Complete Book of Spanish

Nombre_____

Colorful Clothing

Copy each sentence in Spanish on the first line. Write the English meaning on the second line.

1. El vestido es rojo. _____

   _____

2. La camisa es café. _____

   _____

3. El sombrero es morado. _____

   _____

4. La falda es verde. _____

   _____

5. El vestido es rosado. _____

   _____

6. La chaqueta es azul. _____

   _____

7. Los calcetines son amarillos. _____

   _____

8. El cinturón es anaranjado. _____

   _____

9. Las botas son blancas. _____

   _____

Matching Clothes

At the bottom of each picture, write the English word that matches the Spanish and the pictures. Write the Spanish words next to the English at the bottom of the page.

falda	zapatos	pantalones cortos	cinturón
abrigo	calcetines	vestido	botas
guantes	pantalones	chaqueta	blusa
gorro	sandalias	camisa	

1. skirt _____

2. belt _____

3. jacket _____

4. socks _____

5. coat _____

6. shirt _____

7. sandals _____

8. dress _____

9. cap _____

10. pants _____

11. gloves _____

12. boots _____

13. shoes _____

14. blouse _____

15. shorts _____

Clothes Closet

Circle the Spanish words that you find in the puzzle. Write the English meanings at the bottom of the page next to the Spanish words from the puzzle.

v	s	q	o	d	i	t	s	e	v	f	a	o
i	e	a	c	o	y	f	f	n	a	s	g	g
r	n	b	t	j	n	c	l	l	e	i	j	u
x	ó	x	s	o	r	a	d	n	r	q	r	a
s	r	h	u	e	b	a	i	b	l	y	i	n
a	u	t	g	c	n	t	a	l	p	g	b	t
i	t	c	y	g	e	o	a	g	n	z	o	e
l	n	o	m	c	b	o	l	s	o	m	s	s
a	i	v	l	l	k	o	v	a	i	r	x	v
d	c	a	u	e	m	l	n	s	t	m	r	a
n	c	s	z	a	p	a	t	o	s	n	a	o
a	a	k	a	t	e	u	q	a	h	c	a	c
s	g	u	f	a	t	e	z	i	m	a	c	p

Spanish Word	English		Spanish Word	English
abrigo	_____		sandalias	_____
guantes	_____		calcetines	_____
blusa	_____		falda	_____
chaqueta	_____		vestido	_____
pantalones	_____		camisa	_____
botas	_____		gorro	_____
cinturón	_____		zapatos	_____

The Complete Book of Spanish

Face

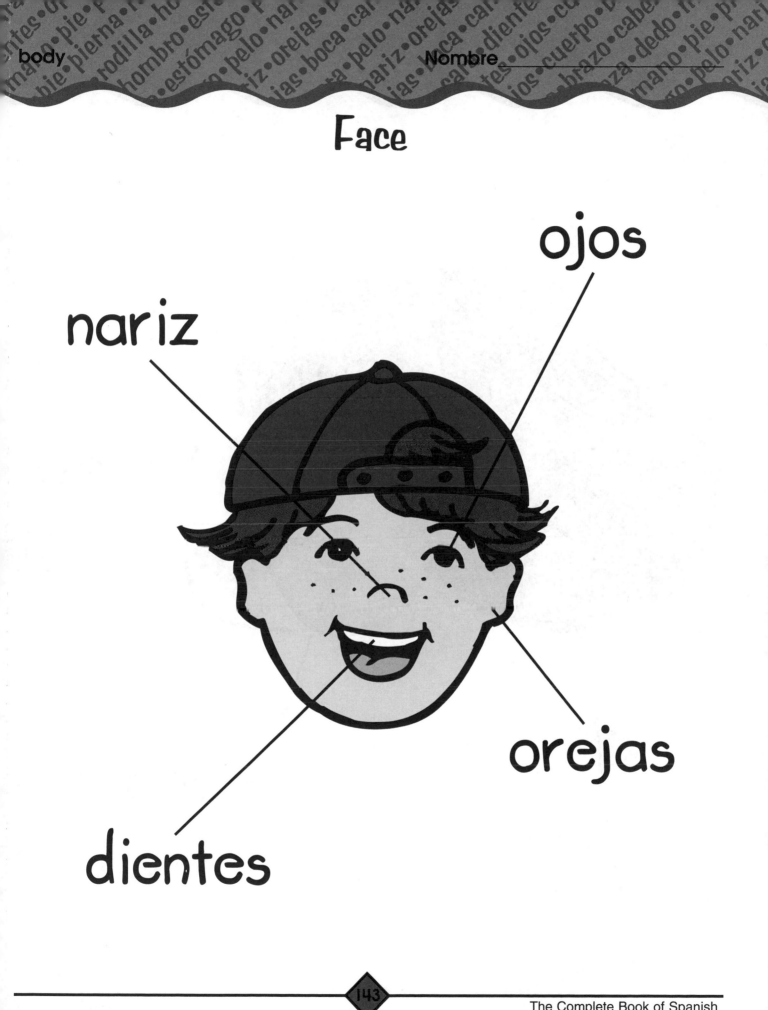

ojos

nariz

orejas

dientes

The Complete Book of Spanish

Face

cara

boca

pelo

What's on Your Face?

Say each word out loud. Copy each word.

▶ pelo

▶ nariz

▶ ojos

▶ orejas

▶ dientes

▶ boca

▶ cara

Which part of your face do you like the best? _____

(Answer in Spanish.)

The Complete Book of Spanish

Face Riddles

Can you guess the answers to the following riddles? Use the size and shape of the letter blocks to write the Spanish word. The answers at the bottom will help you.

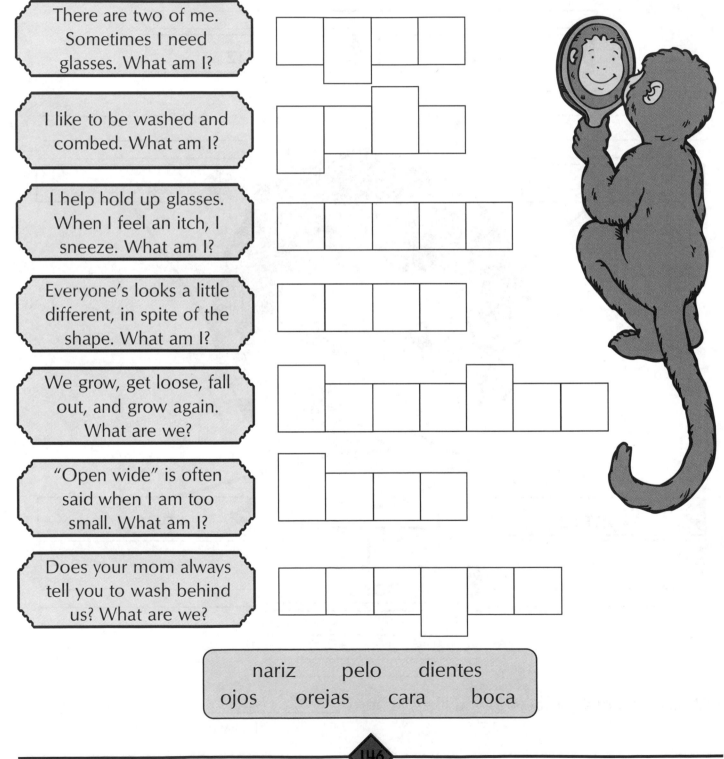

There are two of me. Sometimes I need glasses. What am I?

I like to be washed and combed. What am I?

I help hold up glasses. When I feel an itch, I sneeze. What am I?

Everyone's looks a little different, in spite of the shape. What am I?

We grow, get loose, fall out, and grow again. What are we?

"Open wide" is often said when I am too small. What am I?

Does your mom always tell you to wash behind us? What are we?

| nariz | pelo | dientes |
| ojos | orejas | cara | boca |

The Complete Book of Spanish

A Blank Face

Fill in the blanks with the missing letters. Use the Spanish words below to help you.

| nariz | pelo | dientes | ojos | orejas | cara | boca |

Which word didn't you use? _____

Color each block that has a letter k inside. Do not color the blocks with numbers.
What hidden word did you find? _____

k	5	5	5	5	5	5	5	5	5	5	5	5	5	5
k	5	5	5	5	5	5	5	5	5	5	5	5	5	5
k	5	5	5	5	5	5	5	5	5	5	5	5	5	5
k	k	k	5	k	k	k	5	k	k	k	5	k	k	k	5
k	5	k	5	k	5	k	5	k	5	5	5	k	5	k	5
k	5	k	5	k	5	k	5	k	5	5	5	k	5	k	5
k	k	k	5	k	k	k	5	k	k	k	5	k	k	k	k

Head to Toe

Using the Word Banks, label the parts of the face and body.

Word Bank

cara   ojos   boca   nariz   dientes   orejas   pelo

Word Bank

cuerpo   cabeza   mano   pierna   hombro
brazo   dedo   pie   rodilla   estómago

Diagonal Digits

Circle the Spanish words you find in the word search. Then write the English meanings next to the Spanish words at the bottom of the page.

o	o	b	o	j	o	s	y	f	g	e	r	k	a	z
v	r	p	o	t	k	k	z	m	t	b	s	i	p	a
y	z	e	r	c	e	g	b	i	a	q	z	c	n	n
w	j	p	j	e	a	h	w	s	h	c	q	r	a	i
v	z	e	q	a	u	l	g	d	k	d	e	r	a	s
j	r	l	a	x	s	c	t	s	b	i	i	r	e	d
o	g	o	f	f	v	j	e	h	p	z	a	t	p	m
k	o	i	y	g	r	u	f	s	o	c	n	v	v	w
a	d	h	z	x	r	e	w	r	t	e	p	t	b	m
l	o	f	g	b	k	z	b	a	i	o	o	n	i	w
l	x	p	h	k	r	m	z	d	w	b	m	d	e	n
i	o	j	n	n	o	e	u	f	n	x	r	a	e	v
d	n	f	a	h	b	f	h	s	k	j	e	a	g	d
o	a	f	l	a	a	m	y	b	i	j	x	c	z	o
r	m	i	c	f	v	e	p	e	d	n	n	g	p	o

cara _____

cuerpo _____

brazo _____

ojos _____

cabeza _____

dedo _____

boca _____

mano _____

nariz _____

pierna _____

rodilla _____

dientes _____

hombro _____

estómago _____

orejas _____

pelo _____

Head and Shoulders

Refer to the Word Bank to label each body part in Spanish.

Word Bank

cuerpo	pie
brazo	pierna
cabeza	rodilla
dedo	hombro
mano	estómago

The Complete Book of Spanish

Knees and Toes

Write the Spanish words for the clues in the crossword puzzle.

Word Bank

cuerpo	cabeza	mano	pierna	hombro
brazo	dedo	pie	rodilla	estómago

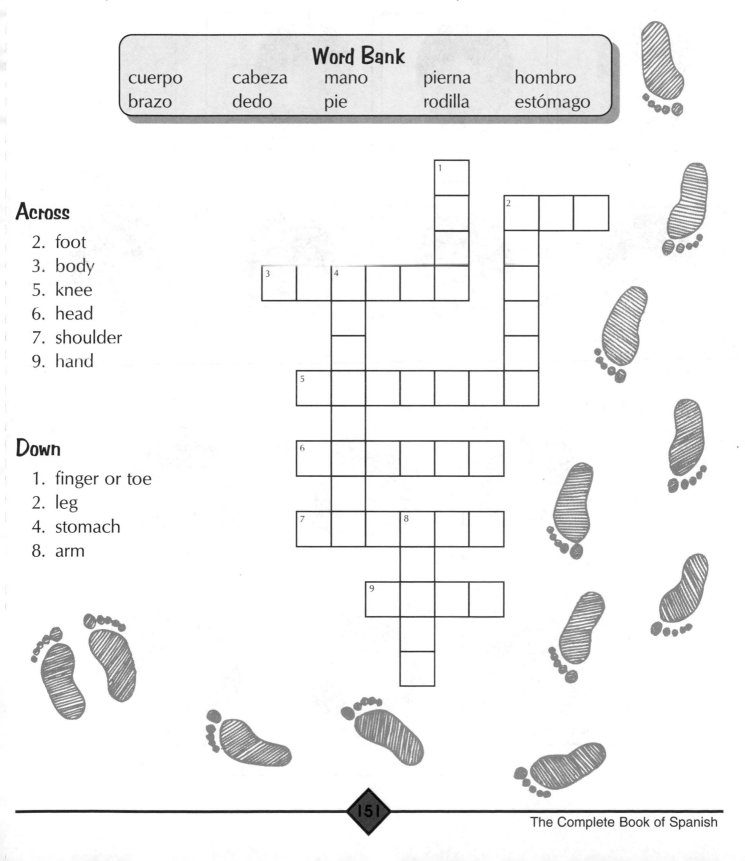

Across

2. foot
3. body
5. knee
6. head
7. shoulder
9. hand

Down

1. finger or toe
2. leg
4. stomach
8. arm

The Complete Book of Spanish

How Are You?

Label each facial feature with a Spanish word from the Word Bank.

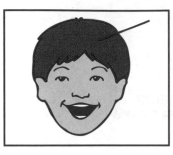 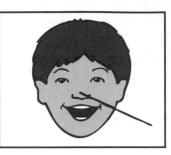 

Word Bank
cara
ojos
boca
nariz
pelo
dientes
orejas

_____

  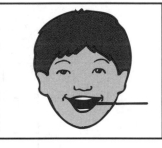 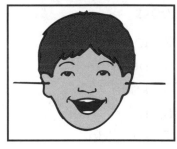

_____

Copy the Spanish word that matches each face pictured.

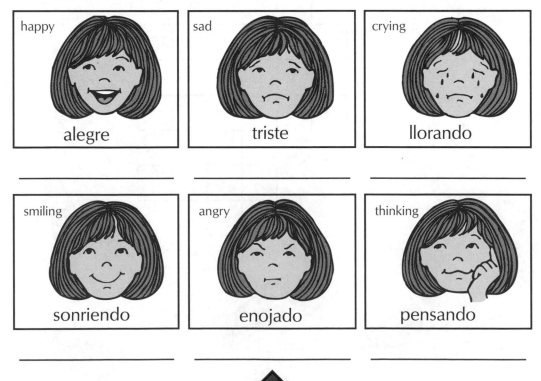

happy	sad	crying
alegre	triste	llorando

_____

smiling	angry	thinking
sonriendo	enojado	pensando

_____

Happy Faces

Write the Spanish for the clue words in the crossword puzzle.

Across

1. sad
3. nose
5. eyes
6. thinking
8. face
11. smiling
13. crying

Down

2. angry
4. happy
7. teeth
9. ears
10. mouth
12. hair

Word Bank

llorando	orejas	sonriendo	ojos
pelo	nariz	triste	cara
dientes	alegre	enojado	boca
pensando			

153

Family

padre

madre

hermano

Nombre_____

Family

hermana

abuela

abuelo

Family Words

Say each family word out loud.

madre		mother
padre		father
hermana		sister
hermano		brother
abuela		grandmother
abuelo		grandfather

The Complete Book of Spanish

My Family

Draw a picture of your family. Color your picture.

Mi familia

Write the correct Spanish word next to each person in your picture above.

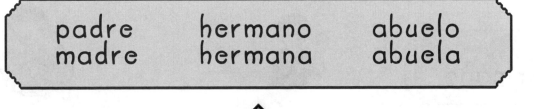

padre   hermano   abuelo
madre   hermana   abuela

Family Word Meanings

Say each word out loud. Circle the picture that shows the meaning of each word.

padre		
hermana		
abuela		
madre		
abuelo		
hermano		

The Complete Book of Spanish

Nombre_____

Matching Family

Cut out a picture of a family out of a magazine. Glue each picture next to the correct word.

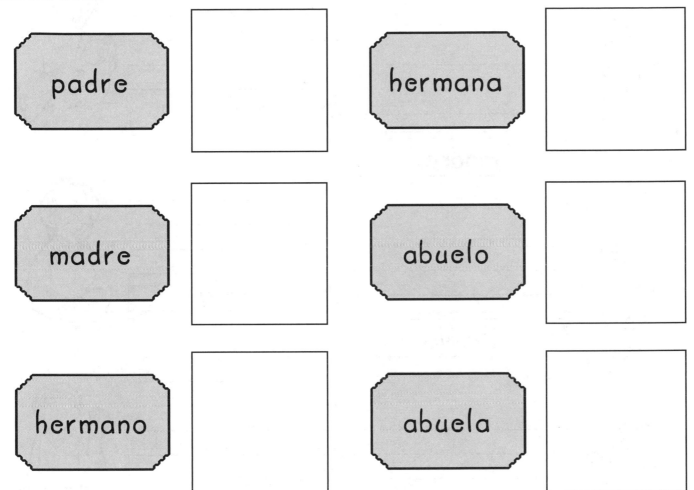

padre		hermana	
madre		abuelo	
hermano		abuela	

Try this: Color each block with a letter inside. Do not color the blocks with numbers. What hidden word did you find? _____

2	2	2	2	2	2	2	2	2	2	2	2	2	m	2	2	2	2	2	2	2
2	2	2	2	2	2	2	2	2	2	2	2	2	m	2	2	2	2	2	2	2
m	m	m	m	m	2	m	m	m	2	2	m	m	m	2	m	m	m	2	m	m	m
m	2	2	2	m	2	m	2	m	2	m	2	m	m	2	m	2	m	2	m	2	m
m	2	m	2	m	2	m	2	m	2	m	2	m	m	2	m	2	2	2	m	m	m
m	2	m	2	m	2	m	2	m	2	m	2	m	m	2	m	2	2	2	m	2	2
m	2	m	2	m	2	m	m	m	2	m	m	m	2	m	m	m	2	m	2	2	2
m	2	m	2	m	2	m	m	m	2	m	m	m	2	m	2	2	2	m	m	m

159

Nombre_____

Family

Copy each word and color the pictures.

> madre

> padre

> abuelo

> abuela

> hermana

> hermano

Let's learn two new words:

> chico   > chica

Nombre_____

Family Crossword

Use the Spanish words at the bottom of the page to fill in your answers.

ACROSS

1. sister
4. father
5. mother
6. girl
7. boy

DOWN

1. brother
2. grandmother
3. grandfather

padre   madre
chico   chica
abuelo   abuela
hermano   hermana

The Complete Book of Spanish

Listen Well

Say each word out loud. Circle the picture for each Spanish word.

padre			
abuelo			
hermana			
chica			
abuela			
madre			
hermano			
chico			

The Complete Book of Spanish

Nombre_____

Family Ties

In each box, copy the Spanish word for family members.

la familia		el hermano	
	family		brother
el padre		la hermana	
	father		sister
la madre		el tío	
	mother		uncle
el hijo		la tía	
	son		aunt
la hija		el abuelo	
	daughter		grandfather
los primos		la abuela	
	cousins		grandmother

Write the Spanish words from above next to the English words.

sister _____   family _____   father _____

grandfather _____   cousins _____   mother _____

grandmother _____   brother _____   daughter _____

uncle _____   aunt _____   son _____

My Family

Write the Spanish word for each clue in the crossword puzzle.

Across

2. son
3. aunt
5. sister
7. grandmother
8. brother
10. cousins

Down

1. mother
2. daughter
4. family
6. grandfather
9. uncle
10. father

Word Bank

familia	hermano	hijo	tía
primos	madre	tío	abuelo
padre	hermana	hija	abuela

Family Tree

Refer to the Word Bank to write the Spanish word that matches each picture.

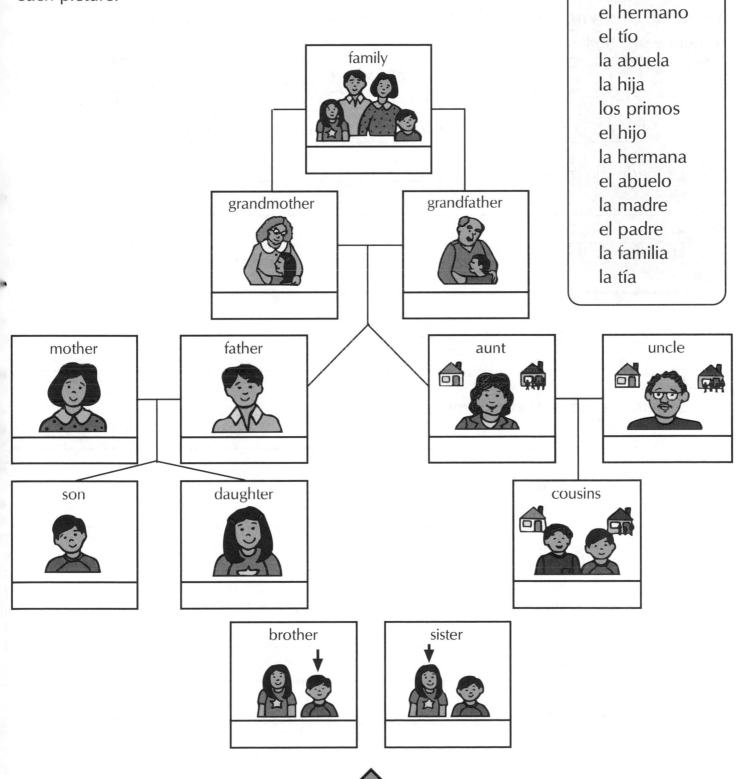

Word Bank

el hermano
el tío
la abuela
la hija
los primos
el hijo
la hermana
el abuelo
la madre
el padre
la familia
la tía

Relationships

How are the following people related? Read the Spanish sentences carefully. Use the words in the Word Bank to complete each sentence. You may use each word only once, and some words may not be used at all. Then, write the English meaning of each sentence on the line below the sentence.

Word Bank

hermano	hija	hermana	padre	tío	primos
abuela	abuelo	familia	hijo	madre	tía

1. La madre de mi madre es mi _____ .

   _____

2. Los hijos de mi tío son mis _____ .

   _____

3. La hija de mi madre es mi _____ .

   _____

4. El hermano de mi padre es mi _____ .

   _____

5. El padre de mi padre es mi _____ .

   _____

6. El hermano de mi tío es mi _____ .

   _____

7. La hermana de mi madre es mi _____ .

   _____

8. La hermana de mi tía es mi _____ .

   _____

Nombre_____

Community

biblioteca

escuela

parque

Community

tienda

casa

museo

Places to Go

Say the Spanish words out loud.

escuela — school

museo — museum

casa — house

tienda — store

biblioteca — library

parque — park

The Complete Book of Spanish

Nombre

Picture This

Say each word out loud. Circle the picture that shows the meaning of each word.

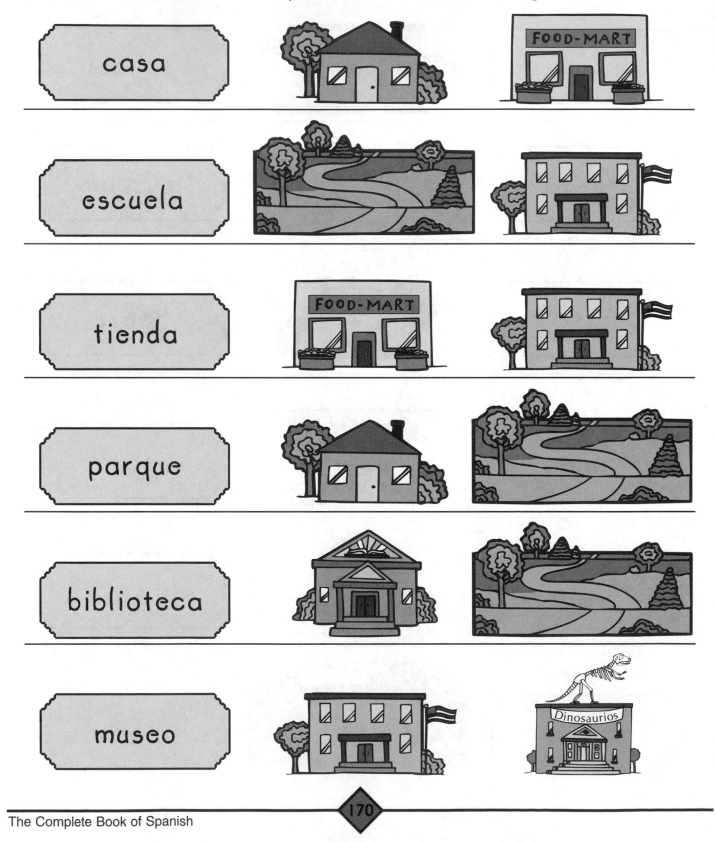

The Complete Book of Spanish

Nombre_____

My Neighborhood

Draw a picture of an imaginary neighborhood. Draw places you have learned about in this book. Add streets, trees, and whatever else you wish to make your neighborhood look nice. Color your picture.

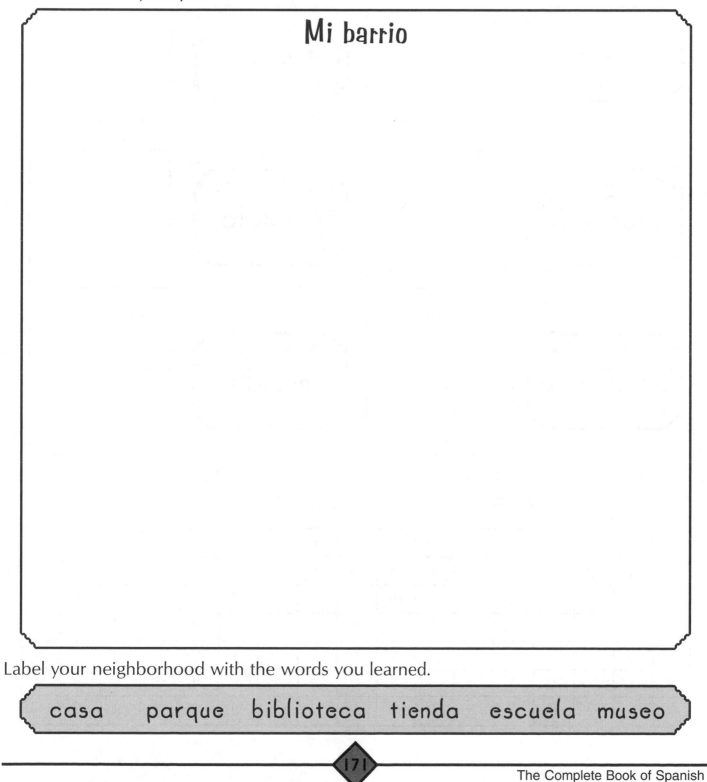

Mi barrio

Label your neighborhood with the words you learned.

casa   parque   biblioteca   tienda   escuela   museo

Places, Please

Cut out pictures that match the words below. Glue each picture next to the correct word.

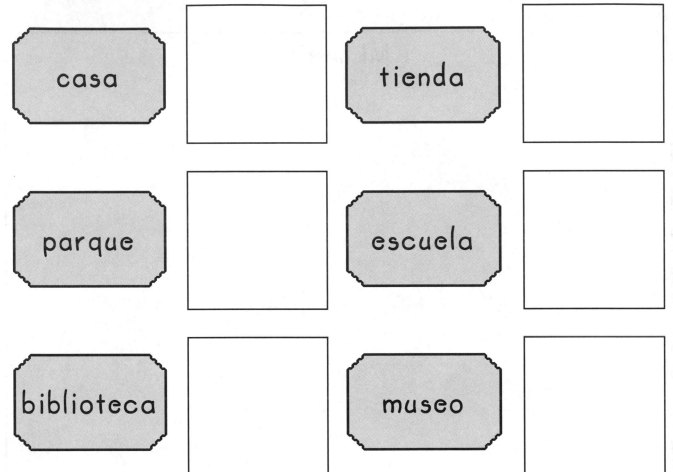

Try this: Color each block with a letter Y inside. Do not color the blocks with numbers. What hidden word did you find? _____

9	9	9	9	9	9	9	9	9	9	9	9	9	9	9	9	9
y	y	y	9	y	y	y	9	9	y	y	y	9	y	y	y	9
y	9	y	9	y	9	y	9	9	y	9	9	9	y	9	y	9
y	9	9	9	y	9	y	9	9	y	9	y	9	y	9	y	9
y	9	y	9	y	9	y	9	9	9	9	y	9	y	9	y	9
y	y	y	9	y	y	y	y	9	y	y	y	9	y	y	y	y
9	9	9	9	9	9	9	9	9	9	9	9	9	9	9	9	9

The Complete Book of Spanish

Places to Go

Say each word out loud. Copy each word and color the picture.

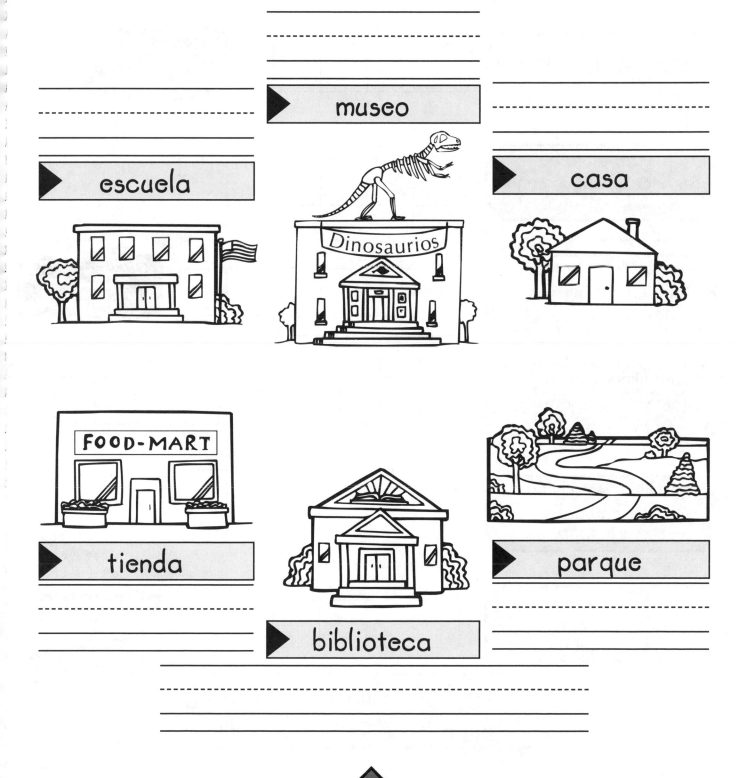

museo

escuela

casa

tienda

biblioteca

parque

Nombre _____

A Place for Riddles

Answer the riddles. Use the size and shape of the letter blocks to write the Spanish words. The answers at the bottom of the page will help you.

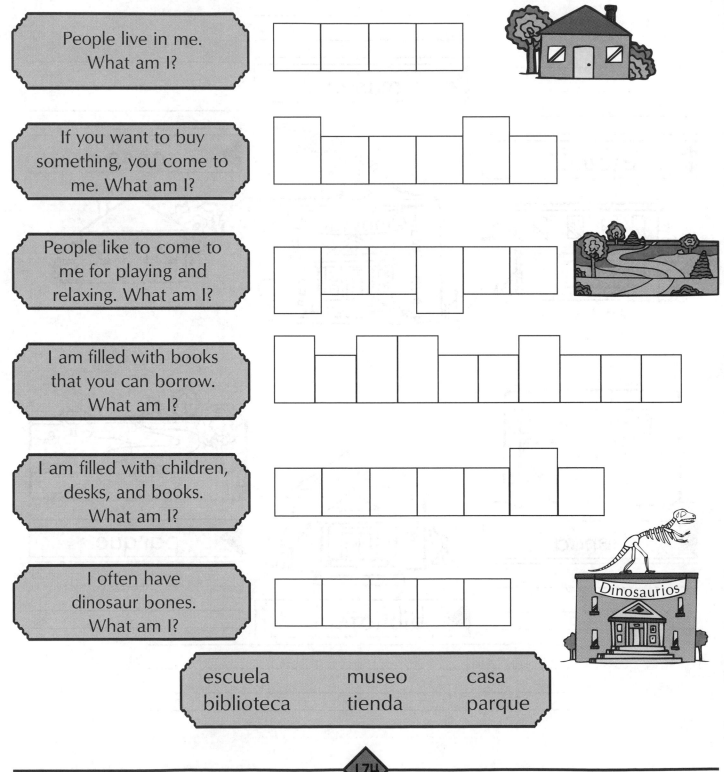

People live in me.
What am I?

If you want to buy something, you come to me. What am I?

People like to come to me for playing and relaxing. What am I?

I am filled with books that you can borrow. What am I?

I am filled with children, desks, and books. What am I?

I often have dinosaur bones. What am I?

Dinosaurios

escuela   museo   casa
biblioteca   tienda   parque

Nombre_____

Our Town

Draw a picture of a town showing community places that you have learned. Label them in Spanish. Use the words at the bottom of the page.

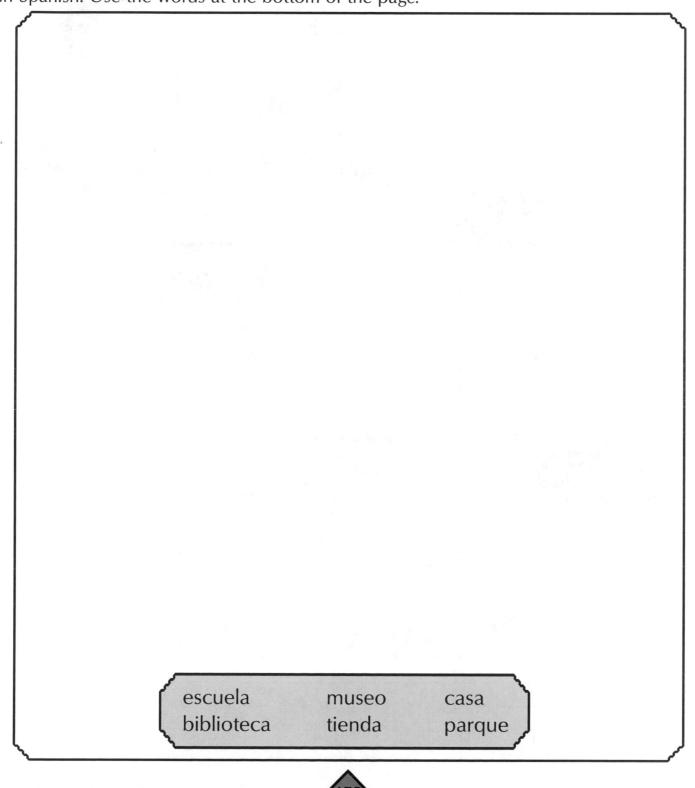

escuela	museo	casa
biblioteca	tienda	parque

Nombre_____

Place Words

Fill in the blanks for place words. Use the Spanish words at the bottom to help you.

escuela museo casa
biblioteca tienda parque

Where Am I?

Refer to the Word Bank and write the Spanish for each place in the community pictured.

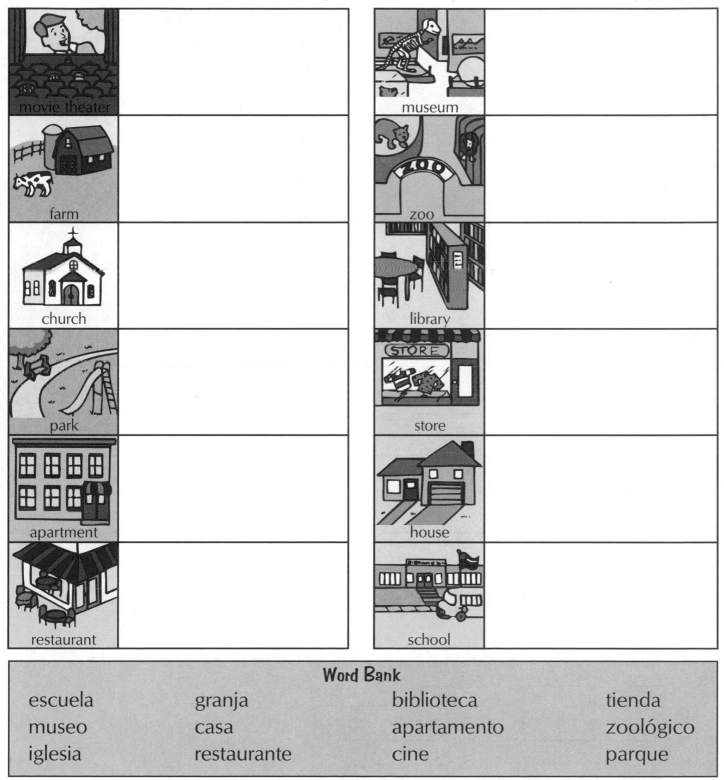

movie theater		museum	
farm		zoo	
church		library	
park		store	
apartment		house	
restaurant		school	

Word Bank			
escuela	granja	biblioteca	tienda
museo	casa	apartamento	zoológico
iglesia	restaurante	cine	parque

The Complete Book of Spanish

Fitting In

Write the Spanish words from the Word Bank in these word blocks. Write the English meanings below the blocks.

Word Bank

granja	escuela	parque
cine	casa	restaurante
museo	iglesia	biblioteca
tienda		

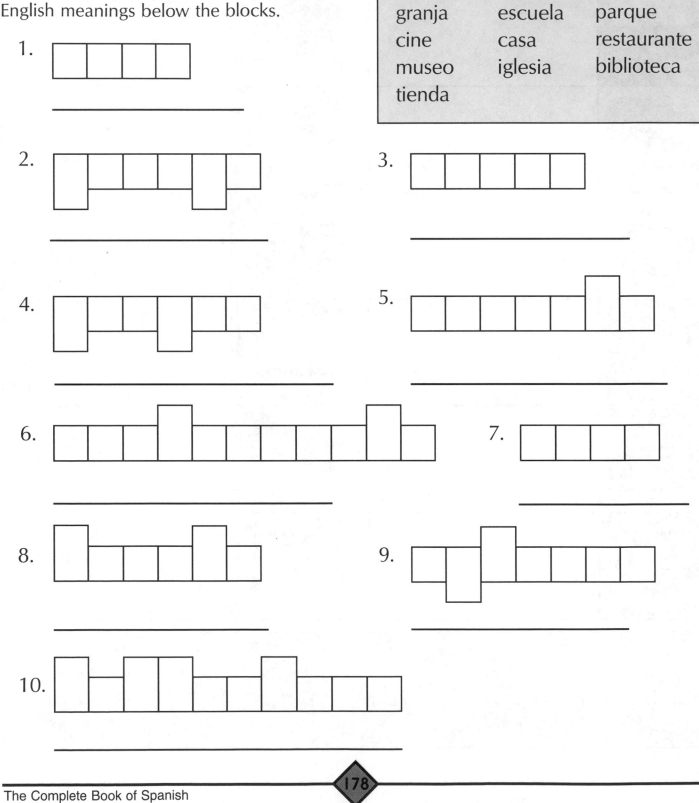

1.

2.

3.

4.

5.

6.

7.

8.

9.

10.

The Complete Book of Spanish

Nombre_____

Name That Place

On your turn roll the die, move your marker, and say the name of the place in Spanish.

• If you can't remember a Spanish word, ask for help and skip a turn.

• The winner is the player to reach the finish first.

• For two to four players.

The Complete Book of Spanish

Around the House

Copy the Spanish words. Then, write the English words below them.

casa		sofá	
_____ _____		_____ _____	

cocina		cama	
_____ _____		_____ _____	

sala		lámpara	
_____ _____		_____ _____	

dormitorio		cuchara	
_____ _____		_____ _____	

Word Bank

couch	kitchen	lamp	spoon
bedroom	bed	house	living room

Around the Block

Write the Spanish words from the Word
Bank that fit in these word blocks. Write
the English below the blocks.

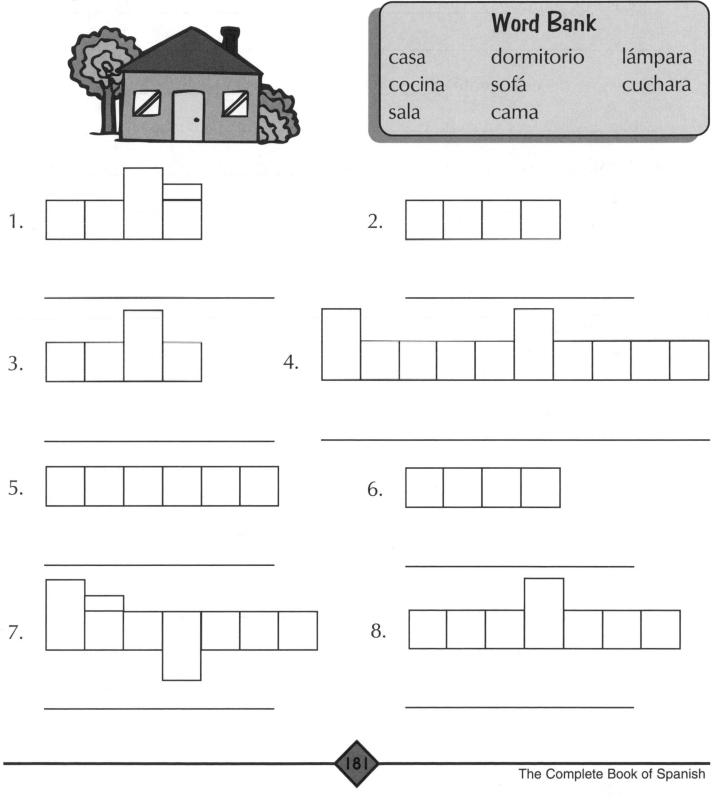

Word Bank

casa	dormitorio	lámpara
cocina	sofá	cuchara
sala	cama	

1.

_____

2.

_____

3.

_____

4.

_____

5.

_____

6.

_____

7.

_____

8.

_____

The Complete Book of Spanish

A Blue House

Copy the sentences in Spanish on the first lines. Write the sentences in English on the second lines.

1. La casa es azul. _____

   _____

2. La sala es de color café. _____

   _____

3. El dormitorio es morado. _____

   _____

4. La cuchara es verde. _____

   _____

5. El sofá es rosado. _____

   _____

6. La cama es azul. _____

   _____

7. La lámpara es amarilla. _____

   _____

Challenge:

La fruta está en la cocina. _____

_____

_____

_____

Nombre_____

Around Town

Write the Spanish words to match the pictures. Write the English next to the Spanish at the bottom of the page.

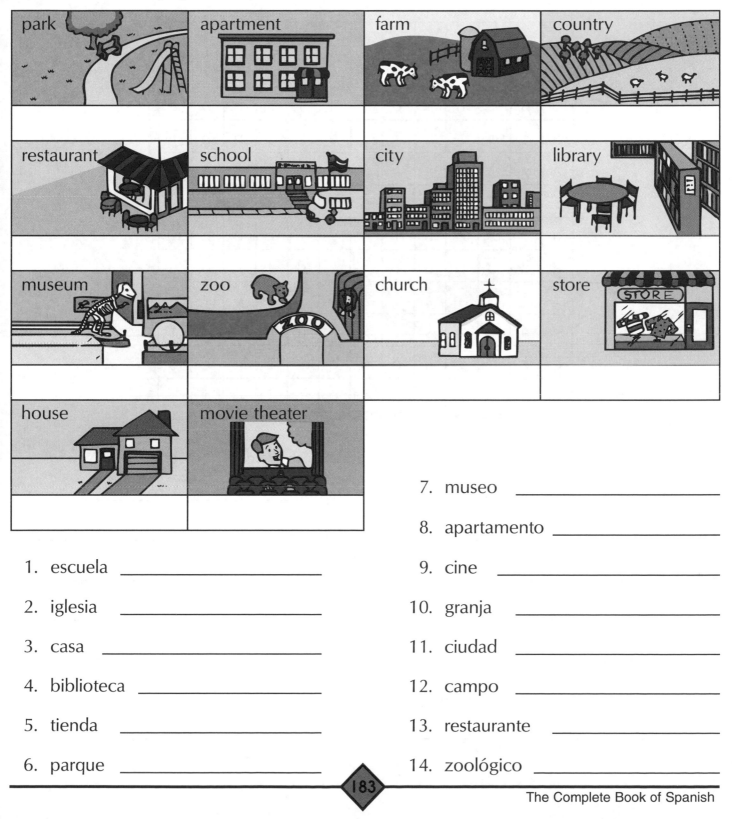

1. escuela _____

2. iglesia _____

3. casa _____

4. biblioteca _____

5. tienda _____

6. parque _____

7. museo _____

8. apartamento _____

9. cine _____

10. granja _____

11. ciudad _____

12. campo _____

13. restaurante _____

14. zoológico _____

The Complete Book of Spanish

Nombre_____

Up the Street

Circle the Spanish community-related words that you find in the word search. Write the English beside the Spanish at the bottom of the page.

t	c	b	e	s	c	u	e	l	a	m	t	a
e	e	i	a	d	n	e	i	t	u	j	j	p
t	n	n	u	n	o	l	a	s	a	n	p	a
n	i	d	a	d	i	y	e	s	a	n	n	r
a	g	l	a	s	a	o	f	r	a	i	l	t
r	l	t	h	e	t	d	g	o	o	r	ñ	a
u	e	z	o	o	l	ó	g	i	c	o	n	m
a	s	q	p	u	i	l	i	c	i	k	b	e
t	i	p	m	a	j	l	o	f	n	o	r	n
s	a	m	a	s	u	x	o	n	e	w	r	t
e	e	d	c	a	e	u	q	r	a	p	e	o
r	o	v	a	c	e	t	o	i	l	b	i	b

Spanish Word	English	Spanish Word	English
escuela	_____	tienda	_____
iglesia	_____	biblioteca	_____
zoológico	_____	ciudad	_____
campo	_____	restaurante	_____
casa	_____	granja	_____
apartamento	_____	cine	_____
museo	_____	parque	_____

Home, Sweet Home

At the bottom of each picture, copy the Spanish word.

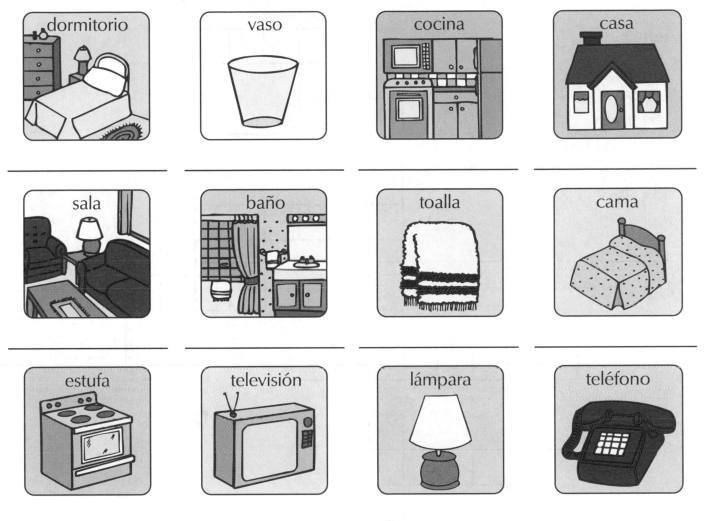

Write the Spanish word after each room or household item.

bathroom _____   lamp _____

towel _____   bed _____

television _____   telephone _____

bedroom _____   stove _____

living room _____   glass _____

kitchen _____   house _____

185

Around the House

Write the Spanish words for the clue words in the crossword puzzle.

Across

2. kitchen
3. lamp
5. towel
8. living room
9. telephone
11. stove

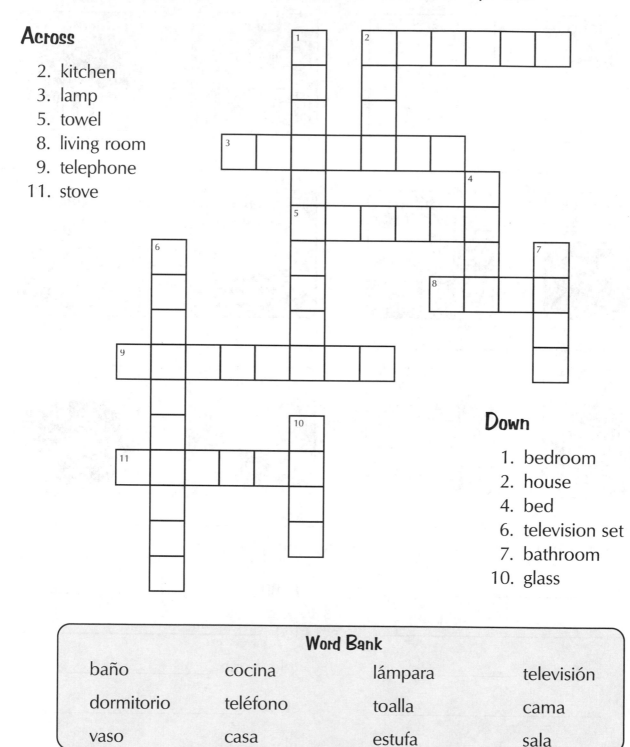

Down

1. bedroom
2. house
4. bed
6. television set
7. bathroom
10. glass

Word Bank

baño	cocina	lámpara	televisión
dormitorio	teléfono	toalla	cama
vaso	casa	estufa	sala

Classroom Objects

libro

lápiz

tijeras

The Complete Book of Spanish

Classroom Objects

borrador

silla

mesa

Nombre_____

Classroom Things

Say each word out loud.

silla		chair
libro		book
mesa		table
lápiz		pencil
tijeras		scissors
borrador		eraser

The Complete Book of Spanish

Matching Objects

Draw a line from the word to the correct picture. Color the picture.

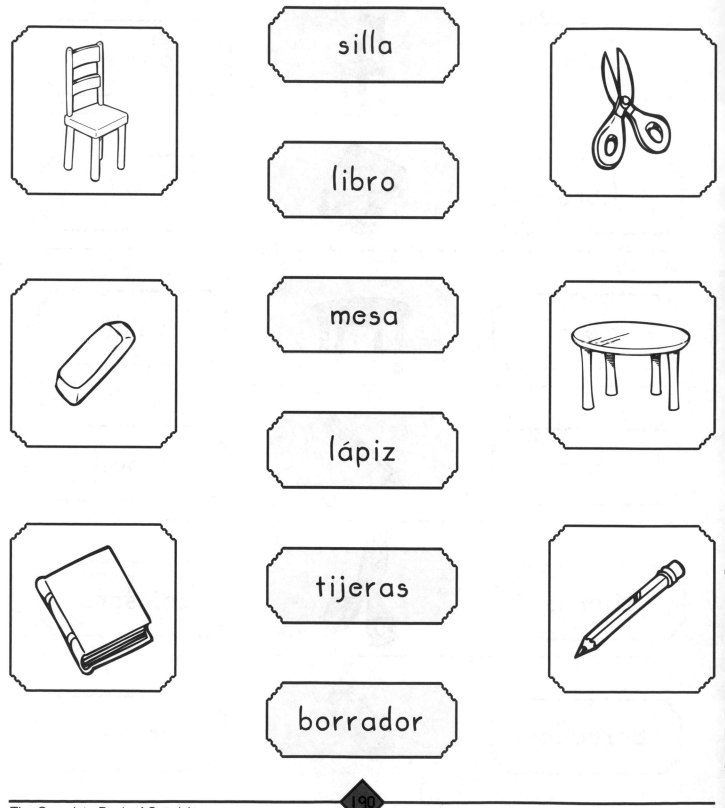

silla

libro

mesa

lápiz

tijeras

borrador

The Complete Book of Spanish

Nombre_____

Draw and Color Your Classroom

Draw and color a picture for each word listed. Which ones do you have in your classroom? Circle them.

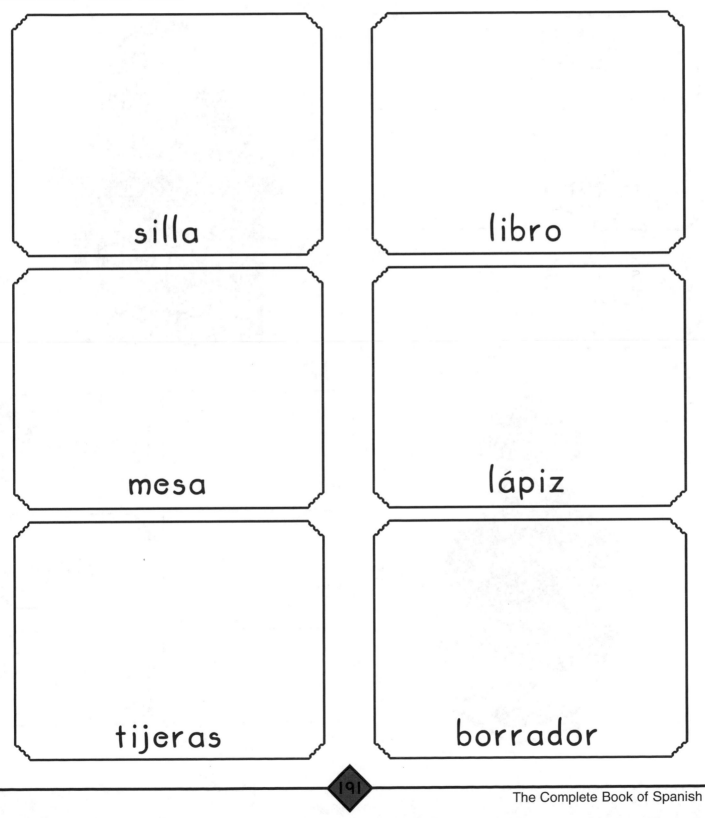

silla

libro

mesa

lápiz

tijeras

borrador

The Complete Book of Spanish

Match Words and Pictures

Cut out pictures from a magazine and glue each picture next to the correct word.

silla

borrador

mesa

lápiz

tijeras

libro

Nombre_____

Classroom Things

Copy each word and color the picture.

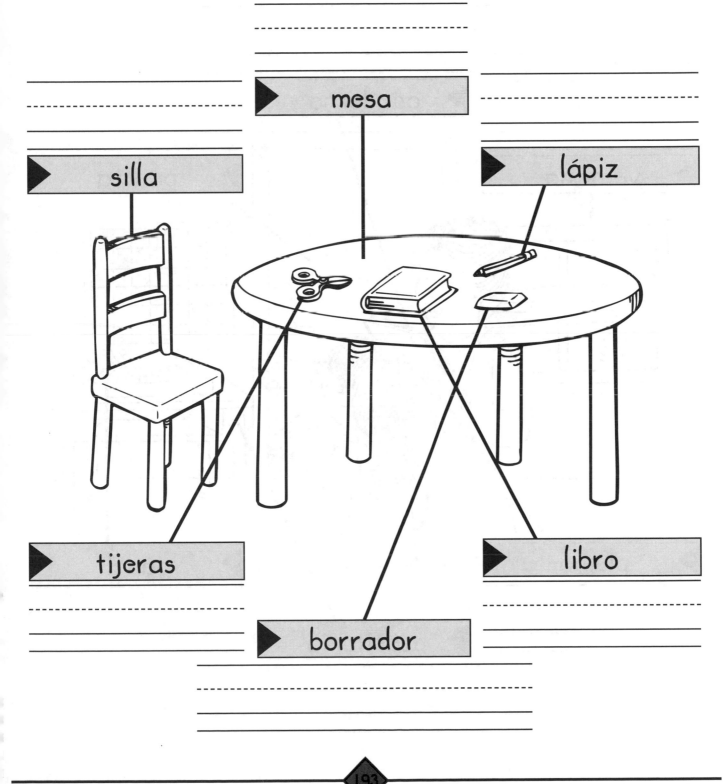

mesa

silla

lápiz

tijeras

libro

borrador

New Classroom Words

Say each word out loud. Copy each word and color the picture.

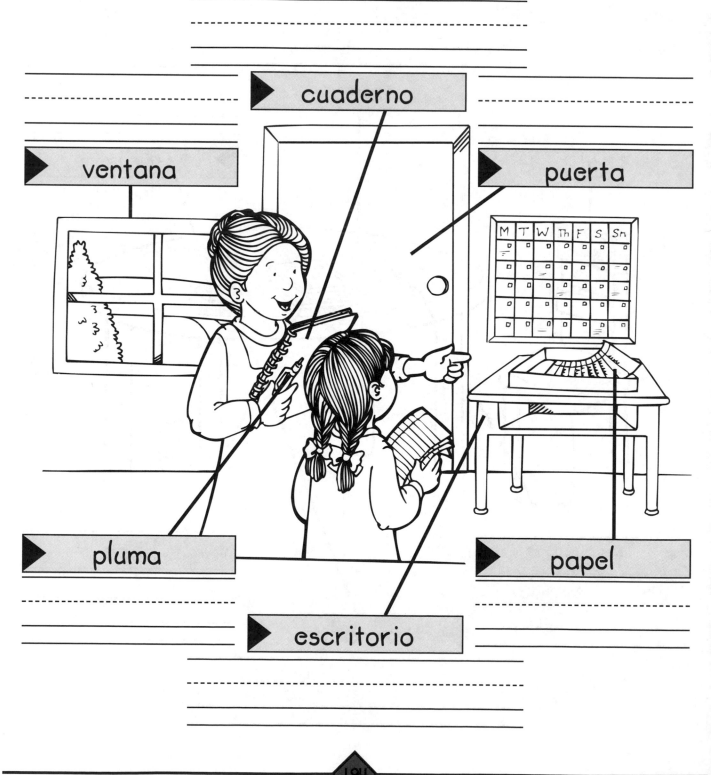

cuaderno

ventana

puerta

pluma

papel

escritorio

Listen Carefully

Say each word out loud. Circle the picture that tells the meaning of each word.

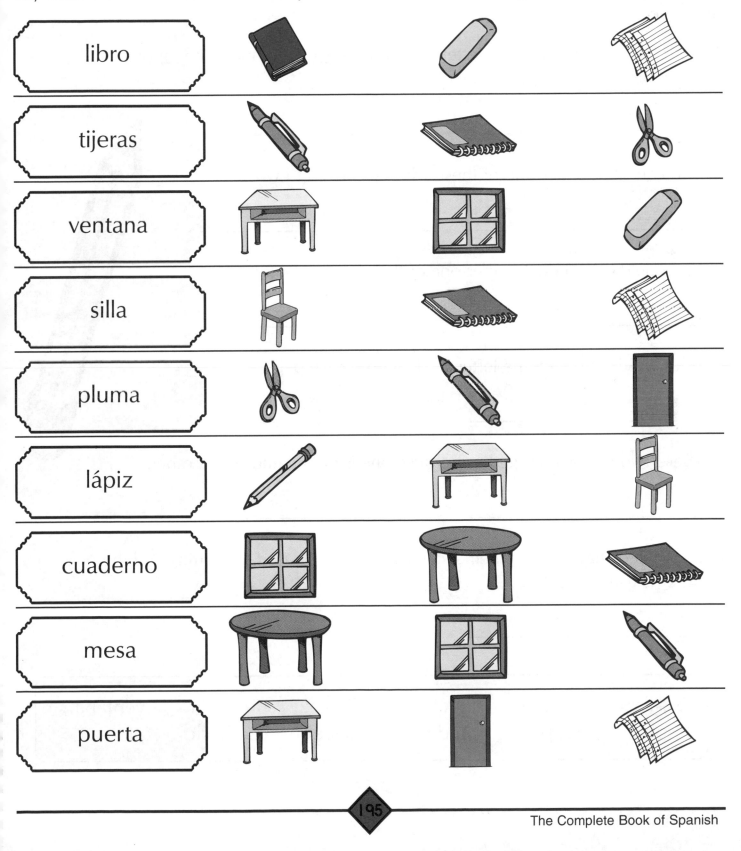

libro

tijeras

ventana

silla

pluma

lápiz

cuaderno

mesa

puerta

The Complete Book of Spanish

Use the Clues

Use the clues and the words at the bottom of the page. Do not use any answer more than once.

1. Both words begin with the letter *p*. You write <u>with</u> one and write <u>on</u> one. What are they?

_____   _____

2. You can sit at either one of these when you need to write.

_____   _____

3. You could exit through either one of these in case of fire.

_____   _____

4. Both words end with the letter *o*. They both have pages.

_____   _____

5. These two words go together because one is on the end of the other.

_____   _____

6. Both words have an *i* as their second letter. One is used for cutting and the other is used for sitting.

_____   _____

silla	mesa	tijeras	libro	borrador	ventana
puerta	lápiz	cuaderno	papel	escritorio	pluma

Nombre_____

Around the Room

In each box, copy the Spanish word for the classroom object pictured.

silla		mesa	
puerta		pluma	
ventana		borrador	
lápiz		cuaderno	
papel		libro	
escritorio		tijeras	

Write the Spanish words from above next to the English words.

window _____ chair _____ table _____

eraser _____ scissors _____ door _____

desk _____ pen _____ notebook _____

paper _____ book _____ pencil _____

The Complete Book of Spanish

Nombre _____

A Fitting Design

Write the Spanish words from the Word Bank that fit in these word blocks. Write the English meanings below the blocks.

Word Bank

ventana	papel	pluma	puerta
borrador	silla	libro	cuaderno
escritorio	tijeras	mesa	lápiz

1.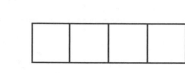

2.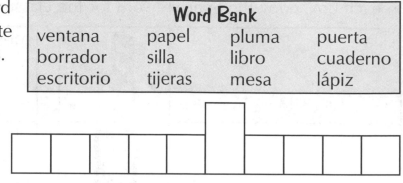

3.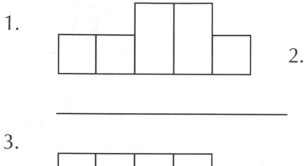

4.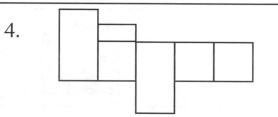

5.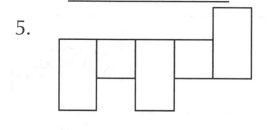

6.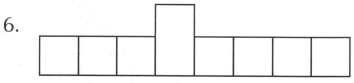

7.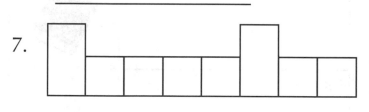

8.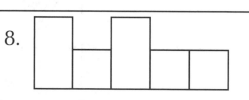

9. 10. 11. 12.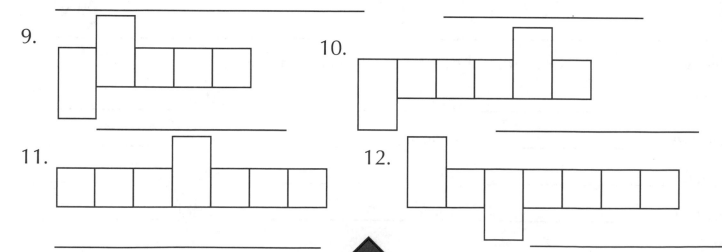

The Complete Book of Spanish

Nombre_____

Where's My Pencil?

Circle the Spanish words that you find in the word search. Then write the English meaning of each word.

w	p	p	a	r	t	m	a	m	u	l	p
r	u	x	f	s	o	t	r	h	h	o	n
x	e	d	e	j	e	d	j	j	i	m	l
o	r	a	h	v	z	m	a	r	a	o	u
o	t	o	f	e	i	f	o	r	m	i	l
n	a	r	t	s	e	t	s	l	r	y	o
r	p	b	f	p	i	a	m	l	h	o	v
e	i	i	g	r	r	e	p	n	d	m	b
d	w	l	c	e	y	e	a	l	l	i	s
a	q	s	j	l	e	f	l	e	p	a	p
u	e	i	l	a	p	i	z	i	m	t	d
c	t	v	e	n	t	a	n	a	i	n	i

Spanish Word	English	Spanish Word	English
ventana	_____	pluma	_____
borrador	_____	libro	_____
escritorio	_____	mesa	_____
papel	_____	puerta	_____
silla	_____	cuaderno	_____
tijeras	_____	lápiz	_____

Classroom Clutter

Draw a picture to illustrate each of the Spanish words. Refer to the Word Bank at the bottom of the page to help you.

silla	ventana
mesa	puerta
tijeras	papel
libro	cuaderno
lápiz	escritorio
borrador	pluma

Word Bank

eraser	door	scissors	pen	window	paper
chair	notebook	pencil	desk	book	table

Nombre _____

Show and Tell

Write the Spanish for each clue in the crossword puzzle.

Across

1. notebook
5. scissors
7. pen
8. eraser
10. pencil
11. table
12. chair

Down

2. desk
3. window
4. book
6. door
9. paper

Word Bank

escritorio	mesa	libro	silla	tijeras	puerta
lápiz	ventana	borrador	cuaderno	papel	pluma

The Complete Book of Spanish

Pencil and Paper

Copy the following sentences in Spanish. Then, write the English meanings.

1. El libro es rojo. _____

_____

2. La silla es de color café. _____

_____

3. El cuaderno es morado. _____

_____

4. La mesa es verde. _____

_____

5. El lápiz es rosado. _____

_____

6. El borrador es amarillo. _____

_____

7. La ventana es azul. _____

_____

8. El escritorio es anaranjado. _____

_____

9. El papel es blanco. _____

_____

Songs and Chants

Diez (veinte) amigos

(to the tune of "Ten Little Fingers")

Uno, dos, tres amigos,
cuatro, cinco, seis amigos,
siete, ocho, nueve amigos,
diez amigos son.

Diez, nueve, ocho amigos
siete, seis, cinco amigos
cuatro, tres, dos amigos,
un amigo es.

Once, doce, trece amigos,
catorce, quince, dieciséis amigos,
diecisiete, dieciocho,
diecinueve amigos,
veinte amigos son.

Community Song

(to the tune of "Here We Go 'Round the Mulberry Bush")

Escuela is school,
museo — museum,
casa is house,
tienda is store,
biblioteca is library,
parque is the park for me!

The Complete Book of Spanish

Songs and Chants

Family Song
(to the tune of "Are You Sleeping?")

Padre — father,
madre — mother,
chico — boy,
chica — girl,
abuelo is grandpa,
abuela is grandma.
Our family, our family.

Hermano — brother,
hermana — sister,
chico — boy,
chica — girl,
padre y madre,
abuelo y abuela.
Our family, our family.

Los días de la semana
(to the tune of "Clementine")

Domingo, lunes,
martes, miércoles,
jueves, viernes, sábado,
domingo, lunes,
martes, miércoles,
jueves, viernes, sábado. (*Repitan*)

Songs and Chants

¡Hola! Means Hello
(to the tune of "London Bridge")

¡Hola! means hello-o-o, hello-o-o, hello-o-o.
¡Hola! means hello-o-o. ¡Hola, amigos!

¡Adiós! Means Good-bye
(to the tune of "London Bridge")

¡Adiós! means goo-ood-bye, goo-ood-bye, goo-ood-bye.
¡Adiós! means goo-ood-bye. ¡Adiós, amigos!

Cinco amigos
(to the tune of "Ten Little Fingers")

Uno, dos, tres, cuatro, cinco,
Uno, dos, tres, cuatro, cinco,
Uno, dos, tres, cuatro, cinco,
Cinco amigos son.

Songs and Chants

Diez amigos

(to the tune of "Ten Little Fingers")

Uno, dos, tres amigos,
cuatro, cinco, seis amigos,
siete, ocho, nueve amigos,
diez amigos son.

Diez, nueve, ocho amigos,
siete, seis, cinco amigos,
cuatro, tres, dos amigos,
un amigo es.

Colors Song

(to the tune of "Twinke, Twinkle Little Star")

Red is rojo,   green is verde,
purple, morado,   brown, café;
yellow, amarillo,   blue, azul,
pink is rosado,   orange, anaranjado;
white is blanco,   black is negro,
colors, colores,   colors, colores.

Songs and Chants

Classroom Objects Song

(to the tune of "The Farmer in the Dell")

A silla is a chair;
A libro is a book;
A mesa is a table in our classroom.

A lápiz is a pencil;
Tijeras is a scissors;
A borrador is an eraser in our classroom.

Clothing Song

(to the tune of "Skip to My Lou")

Camisa — shirt,   pantalones — pants,
vestido — dress,   calcetines — socks,
zapatos — shoes, gorro — cap
These are the clothes that we wear.

Songs and Chants

Food Song

(to the tune of "She'll Be Coming 'Round the Mountain")

Queso is cheese, yum, yum, yum. (clap, clap)
Leche is milk, yum, yum, yum. (clap, clap)
Papa is potato.
Jugo is juice.
Pan is bread, yum, yum, yum! (clap, clap)

Pollo is chicken, yum, yum, yum. (clap, clap)
Ensalada is salad, yum, yum, yum. (clap, clap)
Queso, leche, papa,
jugo, pan, pollo, ensalada,
yum, yum, yum, yum, yum! (clap, clap)

Community Song

(to the tune of "Here We Go 'Round the Mulberry Bush")

Escuela is school,   museo museum;
casa is house,   tienda is store;
biblioteca is library;   parque is the park for me!

Songs and Chants

Name Chant

(snap, clap, snap, clap with the rhythm
 of the question and answer)

Teacher: *¿Cómo te llamas?*

Student: *Me llamo* _____.

(Repeat until everyone has had a turn
answering the question)

Adiós Means Good-bye

(to the tune of "London Bridge")

Adiós means goo-ood-bye,
        goo-ood-bye,
        goo-ood-bye.
Adiós means goo-ood-bye.
¡Adiós, amigos!

¡Hasta luego! — see you later,
            see you later,
            see you later.
¡Hasta luego! — see you later.
¡Hasta luego, amigos!

Diez (veinte) amigos

(to the tune of "Ten Little Fingers")

*Uno, dos, tres amigos,
cuatro, cinco, seis amigos,
siete, ocho, nueve amigos,
diez amigos son.*

*Diez, nueve, ocho amigos
siete, seis, cinco amigos
cuatro, tres, dos amigos,
un amigo es.*

*Once, doce, trece amigos,
catorce, quince, dieciséis amigos,
diecisiete, dieciocho,
diecinueve amigos,
veinte amigos son.*

Colors Song

(to the tune of "Twinkle, Twinkle, Little Star")

Red is *rojo;* green is *verde;*
purple, *morado;* brown, *café;*
yellow, *amarillo;* blue, *azul;*
pink, *rosado;* orange, *anaranjado;*
white is *blanco;* black is *negro;*
colors, *colores;* colors, *colores.*

The Complete Book of Spanish

Songs and Chants

Classroom Objects Song

(to the tune of "The Farmer in the Dell")

A *silla* is a chair,
a *libro* is a book,
a *mesa* is a table in our classroom.

A *lápiz* is a pencil,
tijeras are scissors,
a *borrador* is an eraser in our classroom.

Ventana is a window,
cuaderno is a notebook,
papel is paper in our classroom.

A *puerta* is a door,
a *pluma* is a pen,
escritorio is a desk in our classroom.

Face Song

(to the tune of "Here We Go 'Round the Mulberry Bush")

Ojos — eyes, *boca* — mouth,
nariz — nose, *dientes* — teeth,
orejas — ears, *pelo* — hair,
cara is my face.

Food Song

(to the tune of "She'll Be Coming 'Round the Mountain")

Part 1

Queso is cheese, yum, yum, yum (clap, clap)
leche is milk, yum, yum, yum (clap, clap)
papa is potato, *jugo* is juice, *pan* is bread,
yum, yum, yum! (clap, clap)

Pollo is chicken, yum, yum, yum (clap, clap)
ensalada is salad, yum, yum, yum
(clap, clap)
queso, leche, papa, jugo, pan, pollo, ensalada,
yum, yum, yum, yum, yum! (clap, clap)

Part 2

Sandwich is sandwich, yum, yum, yum
(clap, clap)
manzana is apple, yum, yum, yum
(clap, clap)
sopa is soup, *agua* is water, *carne* is meat,
yum, yum, yum! (clap, clap)

Naranja is orange, yum, yum, yum
(clap, clap)
plátano is banana, yum, yum, yum
(clap, clap)
sandwich, manzana, sopa, agua,
carne, naranja, plátano,
yum, yum, yum, yum, yum! (clap, clap)

The Complete Book of Spanish

Songs and Chants

Family Song

(to the tune of "Are You Sleeping?")

Padre — father,
madre — mother,
chico — boy,
chica — girl,
abuelo is grandpa,
abuela is grandma.
Our family, our family.

Hermano — brother,
hermana — sister,
chico — boy,
chica — girl,
padre y madre,
abuelo y abuela.
Our family, our family.

Clothing Song

(to the tune of "Skip to My Lou")

Camisa — shirt, *pantalones* — pants,
vestido — dress, *calcetines* — socks,
zapatos — shoes, *gorro* — cap.
These are the clothes that we wear.

Chaqueta — jacket, *botas* — boots,
abrigo — dress, *falda* — skirt,
guantes are gloves. What did we forget?
Pantalones cortos are shorts.

Animals Song

(to the tune of "This Old Man")

Gato — cat,
perro — dog,
pájaro is a flying bird,
pez is a fish, and
pato is a duck,
culebra is a slinky snake.

Songs and Chants

Community Song

(to the tune of "Here We Go 'Round the Mulberry Bush")

Escuela is school,
museo — museum,
casa is house,
tienda is store,
biblioteca is library,
parque is the park for me!

Alphabet Song

(to the tune of "B-I-N-G-O")

A   B   C   D   E   F   G
(There was   a   farmer had   a   dog)

H   I   J   K
(and Bin-   go   was his   name-o.)

L   M   N   Ñ   O
(B   I   N   G   O)

P   Q   R   S   T
(B   I   N   G   O)

U   V   W
(B   I   N G O)

X   Y   Z
(and   Bingo was his name-o.)

Songs

¡Hola, chicos!

(to the tune of "Goodnight Ladies")

¡Hola, chico! ¡Hola, chica!
¡Hola, chicos! ¿Cómo están hoy?
¡Hola, chico! ¡Hola, chica!
¡Hola, chicos! ¿Cómo están hoy?

Los días de la semana

(to the tune of "Clementine")

Domingo, lunes,
martes, miércoles,
jueves, viernes, sábado,
domingo, lunes,
martes, miércoles,
jueves, viernes, sábado. (*Repitan*)

213

The Complete Book of Spanish

Songs

Cumpleaños feliz
(to the tune of "Happy Birthday")

Cumpleaños feliz,
Cumpleaños feliz,
Te deseamos todos,
Cumpleaños feliz.

Así me lavo las manos
(to the tune of "Here We Go Round the Mulberry Bush")

Así me lavo las manos, las manos, las manos   (Use hand motions to show hand washing)

Así me lavo las manos, por la mañana.

Así me lavo la cara, la cara, la cara   (Use hand motions to show face washing)

Así me lavo la cara, por la mañana.

Así me lavo los pies, los pies, los pies   (Use different body parts that students pick)

(los brazos, el estómago, etc.)

Songs

Fray Felipe

(to the tune of "Are You Sleeping?")

Fray Felipe, Fray Felipe, ¿Duermes tú, duermes tú?
Toca la campana, toca la campana, tan, tan, tan, tan, tan, tan.

Fray Francisco, Fray Francisco, ¿Duermes tú, duermes tú?
Toca la campana, toca la campana, tan, tan, tan, tan, tan, tan.

Christmas Carols

Cascabeles

("Jingle Bells")

O, que felicidad caminar en un trineo
por los caminos que blancos ya están.
Nos paseamos con gritos de alegría,
con cantos y risas de dicha caminamos.
O, cascabeles, cascabeles, tra la la la la,
qué alegría todo el día, tra la la la la.
Cascabeles, cascabeles, tra la la la la,
qué alegría todo el día, tra la la la la.

Noche de paz

("Silent Night")

Noche de paz, noche de amor,
todo duerme en derredor.
Entre los astros que esparcen la luz,
bella anunciando al niño Jesús.
Brilla la estrella de paz,
Brilla la estrella de paz.
Noche de paz, noche de amor,
oye humilde el fiel pastor.
Coros celestes que anuncian salud,
gracias y glorias en gran plenitud.
Por nuestro buen Redentor,
Por nuestro buen Redentor.

Christmas Carols

Pueblecito de Belén

("Oh, Little Town of Bethlehem")

O, pueblecito de Belén, la cuna de Jesús,
bendito pueblo de Belén, la cuna de Jesús.
El Rey tan adorado, el santo Redentor,
el Rey que vino al mundo, a darnos paz y amor.

The Complete Book of Spanish

Chants

Body Chant

Cabeza, hombros, rodillas, dedos, rodillas, dedos, rodillas, dedos
Cabeza, hombros, rodillas, dedos
Ojos, orejas, boca, nariz.

Number Chant

Dos y dos son cuatro, cuatro y dos son seis, seis y dos son ocho, y ocho más, dieciséis.
(Two and two are four, four and two are six, six and two are eight, and eight more, sixteen.)

Clothing Chant

Abrigo rosado, vestido blanco,	Pink coat, white dress,
camisa café, sombrero morado,	brown shirt, purple hat,
blusas verdes, pantalones rojos,	green blouses, red pants,
botas azules, zapatos negros.	blue boots, black shoes.

Adjective Chant

La casa es grande, la mesa—pequeña,	The house is big, the table—small,
la puerta—cerrada, la ventana abierta.	the door—closed, the window—open.

Papa Chant

Yo como una papa, no como a mi papá.
   I eat a potato, I don't eat my dad.
Una papa es comida, un papá es un padre.
   A *papa* is a potato, a *papá* is a father.

*Due to differences in languages, literal translations of chants may lose meaning and/or the sense of rhythm.

Chants

The Pledge of Allegiance

Juro fidelidad a la bandera de los Estados Unidos de América, y a la república que representa, una nación bajo Dios, indivisible, con libertad y justicia para todos.

Vowel Chant

A, E, I, O, U ¡Más sabe el burro que tú!   A, E, I, O, U ¿Cuántos años tienes tú?
(A, E, I, O, U A donkey knows more than you! A, E, I, O, U How old are you?)

Number Chant

Dos y dos son cuatro, cuatro y dos son seis, seis, y dos son ocho, y ocho más, dieciséis.
(Two and two are four, four and two are six, six and two are eight, and eight more, sixteen)

Clothing Chant

Abrigo gris, vestido blanco,   Gray coat, white dress,
camisa café, sombrero morado,   brown shirt, purple hat,
blusas verdes, pantalones rojos,   green blouses, red pants,
botas azules, zapatos negros.   blue boots, black shoes.

Body Chant

Cabeza, hombros, rodillas y dedos, rodillas y dedos, rodillas y dedos
Cabeza, hombros, rodillas y dedos
Ojos, orejas, boca, y nariz.

*Due to differences in languages, literal translations of chants may lose meaning and/or the sense of rhythm.

The Complete Book of Spanish

Learning Cards

In this section, students will be able to review the topics they have learned earlier in this book. Beginning on page 221, students will be able to cut out and create illustrated books with the vocabulary words from *The Complete Book of Spanish*.

Beginning on page 267, students can cut out flashcards with a Spanish word on one side and the definition in English on the other side. These flash cards are ideal for both individual and group practice.

Learning Cards Table of Contents

Illustrated Books

Flashcards

Introductions and Greetings

¡Hola!

¿Cómo te llamas?

Me llamo

¡Adiós!

¿Cómo estás?

bien

This page is intentionally left blank.

Introductions and Greetings

mal

así, así

¿Cuántos años tienes?

Tengo _____ años.

sí

no

This page is intentionally left blank.

Introductions and Greetings

por favor

gracias

amigo

amiga

amigos

¡Hasta luego!

This page is intentionally left blank.

Numbers

0 cero

1 uno

2 dos

3 tres

4 cuatro

5 cinco

This page is intentionally left blank.

Numbers and The Face (cara)

6 seis

7 siete

8 ocho

9 nueve

10 diez

cara

This page is intentionally left blank.

Numbers

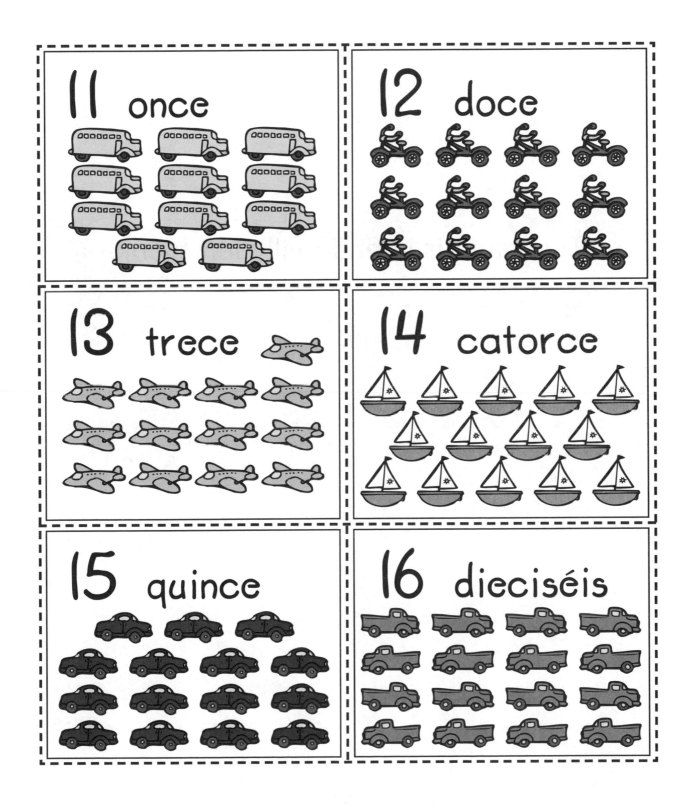

This page is intentionally left blank.

Numbers and Family

17 diecisiete

18 dieciocho

19 diecinueve

20 veinte

hermano

hermana

This page is intentionally left blank.

Family

padre

madre

hermano

hermana

abuelo

abuela

This page is intentionally left blank.

The Face

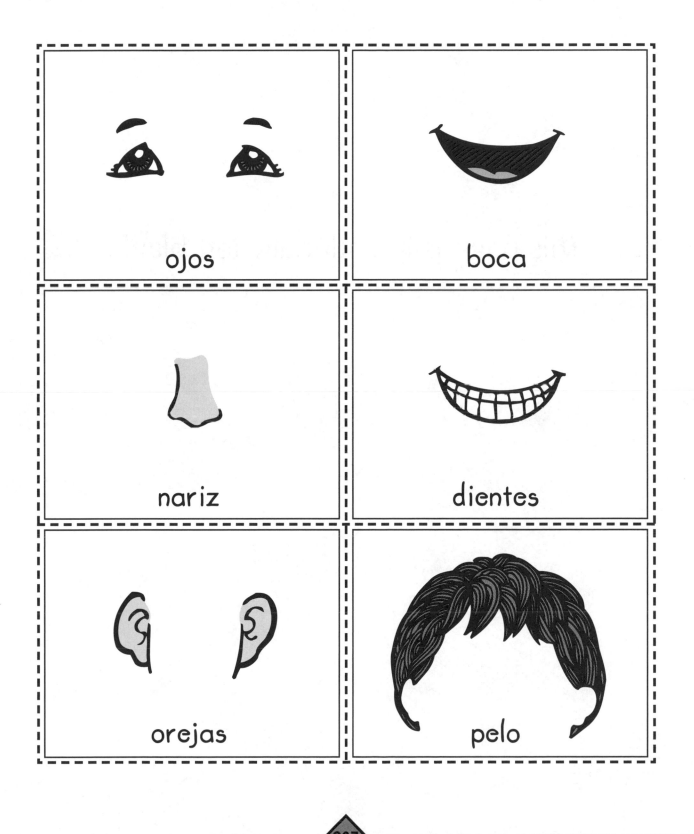

ojos

boca

nariz

dientes

orejas

pelo

The Complete Book of Spanish

This page is intentionally left blank.

Colors

rojo

azul

verde

anaranjado

morado

amarillo

This page is intentionally left blank.

Colors and Food

café

negro

blanco

rosado

pollo

queso

This page is intentionally left blank.

Food

ensalada

pan

jugo

leche

papa

naranja

The Complete Book of Spanish

This page is intentionally left blank.

Nombre_____

Food

carne

plátano

sopa

agua

sandwich

manzana

The Complete Book of Spanish

This page is intentionally left blank.

Classroom Objects

silla

mesa

tijeras

libro

lápiz

borrador

This page is intentionally left blank.

Classroom Objects

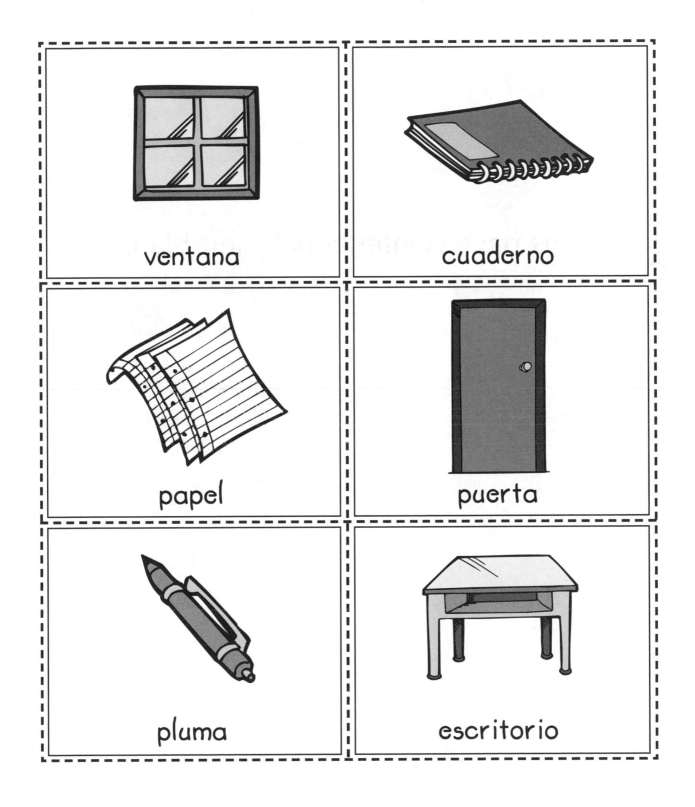

ventana

cuaderno

papel

puerta

pluma

escritorio

This page is intentionally left blank.

Clothing

camisa

pantalones

vestido

calcetines

zapatos

gorro

This page is intentionally left blank.

Clothing

chaqueta

pantalones cortos

botas

guantes

falda

abrigo

This page is intentionally left blank.

Animals

gato

perro

pájaro

pez

pato

culebra

This page is intentionally left blank.

Community

escuela

tienda

museo

biblioteca

casa

parque

This page is intentionally left blank.

Nombre_____

Cover Directions

Cut out the ten covers, one cover per unit.

This page is intentionally left blank.

Me llamo

_____

My

Book

Me llamo

_____

My

Book

This page is intentionally left blank.

Me llamo

_____

My

Book

Me llamo

_____

My

Book

Me llamo

_____

My

Book

This page is intentionally left blank.

Me llamo

_____

My

Book

Me llamo

_____

My

Book

Me llamo

_____

My

Book

This page is intentionally left blank.

uno

cuatro

dos

cinco

tres

seis

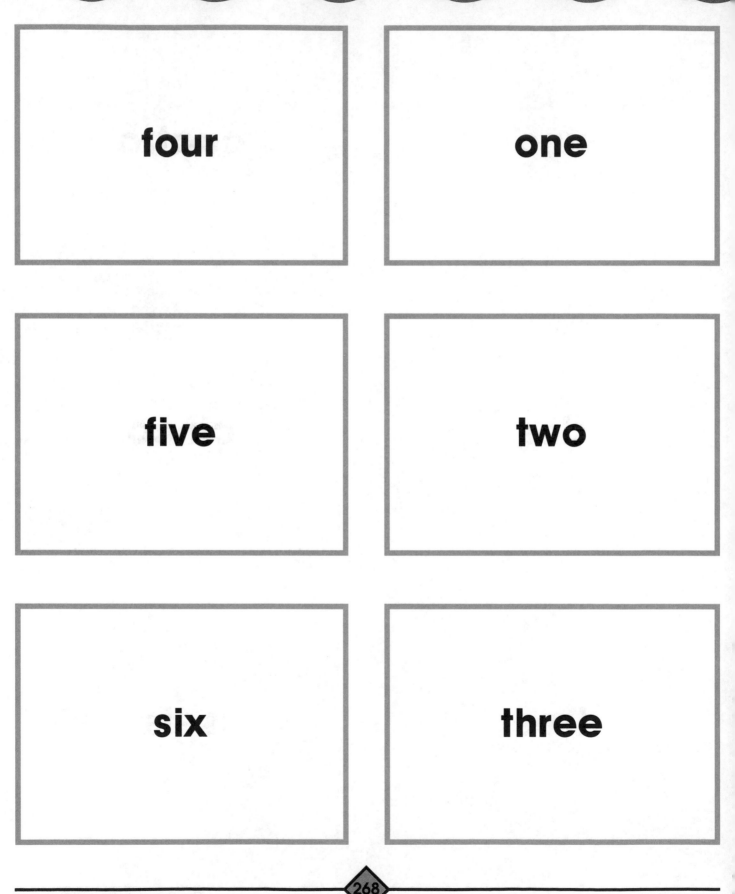

four

one

five

two

six

three

The Complete Book of Spanish

siete

diez

ocho

once

nueve

doce

ten

seven

eleven

eight

twelve

nine

trece

dieciséis

catorce

diecisiete

quince

dieciocho

sixteen

thirteen

seventeen

fourteen

eighteen

fifteen

diecinueve

veintidós

veinte

veintitrés

veintiuno

veinticuatro

twenty-two

nineteen

twenty-three

twenty

twenty-four

twenty-one

veinticinco

las doce

Vamos a contar.

la una

¿Qué hora es?

las dos

twelve o'clock

twenty-five

one o'clock

Let's count.

two o'clock

What time is it?

las tres

las seis

las cuatro

las siete

las cinco

las ocho

six o'clock

three o'clock

seven o'clock

four o'clock

eight o'clock

five o'clock

las nueve

hora

las diez

minuto

las once

segundo

hour

nine o'clock

minute

ten o'clock

second

eleven o'clock

levántense

cierren

siéntense

cállense

abran

pónganse

close

stand up

be quiet

sit down

line up

open

Nombre_____

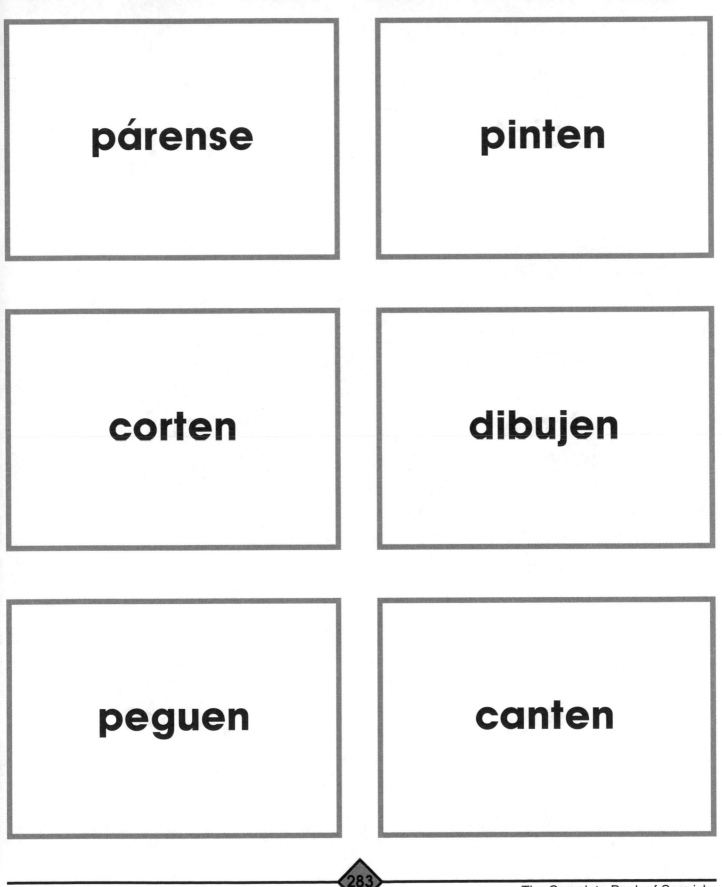

párense

pinten

corten

dibujen

peguen

canten

Nombre_____

paint	**stop**
draw	**cut**
sing	**paste**

saquen

contar

mirar

escribir

escuchar

leer

to count

take out

to write

to look

to read

to listen

Nombre_____

comer

limpiar

hablar

dormir

beber

tocar

to clean

to eat

to sleep

to speak

to touch

to drink

dar

por favor

hola

gracias

adiós

vengan aquí

please

to give

thank you

hello

come here

good-bye

anden por favor

¿Cómo te llamas?

sí

¿Cómo estás?

¿Hablas español?

¿Qué día es hoy?

What is
your name?

please walk

How are you?

yes

What day
is today?

Do you speak
Spanish?

Estoy bien.

¡Buenos días!

Hoy es lunes.

¡Buenas tardes!

¡Mucho gusto!

¡Buenas noches!

Good morning!

I am fine.

Good afternoon!

Today is Monday.

Good night!

Pleased to meet you!

¡Hasta luego!

miércoles

lunes

jueves

martes

viernes

Wednesday

See you later!

Thursday

Monday

Friday

Tuesday

sábado

febrero

domingo

marzo

enero

abril

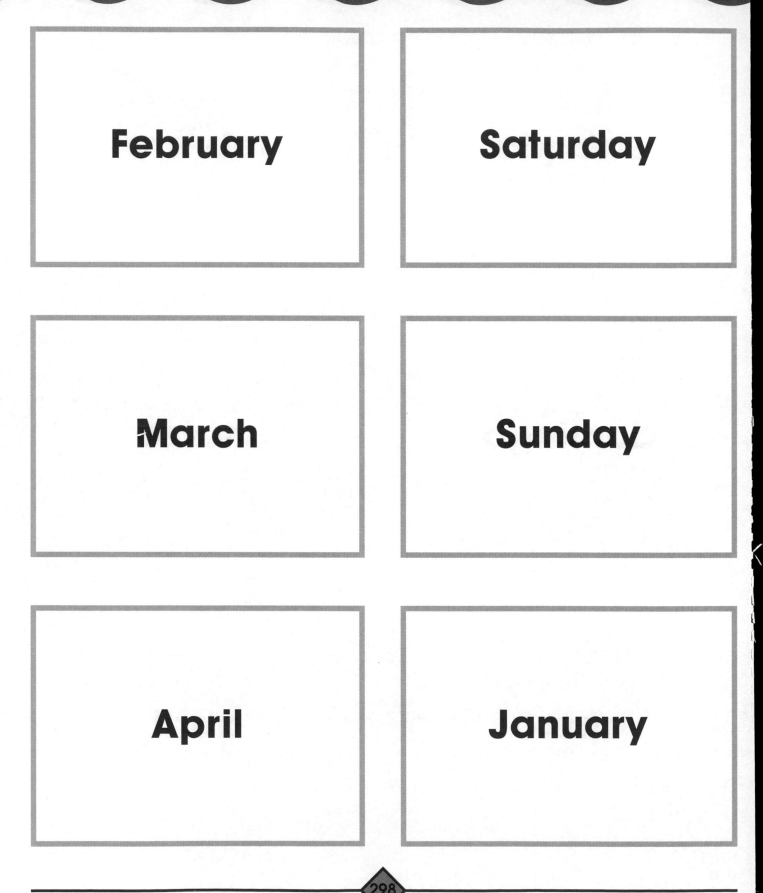

February

Saturday

March

Sunday

April

January

mayo

agosto

junio

septiembre

julio

octubre

August

May

September

June

October

July

noviembre	**verde**
diciembre	**anaranjado**
rojo	**amarillo**

green

November

orange

December

yellow

red

azul

blanco

morado

rosado

negro

de color café

Nombre_____

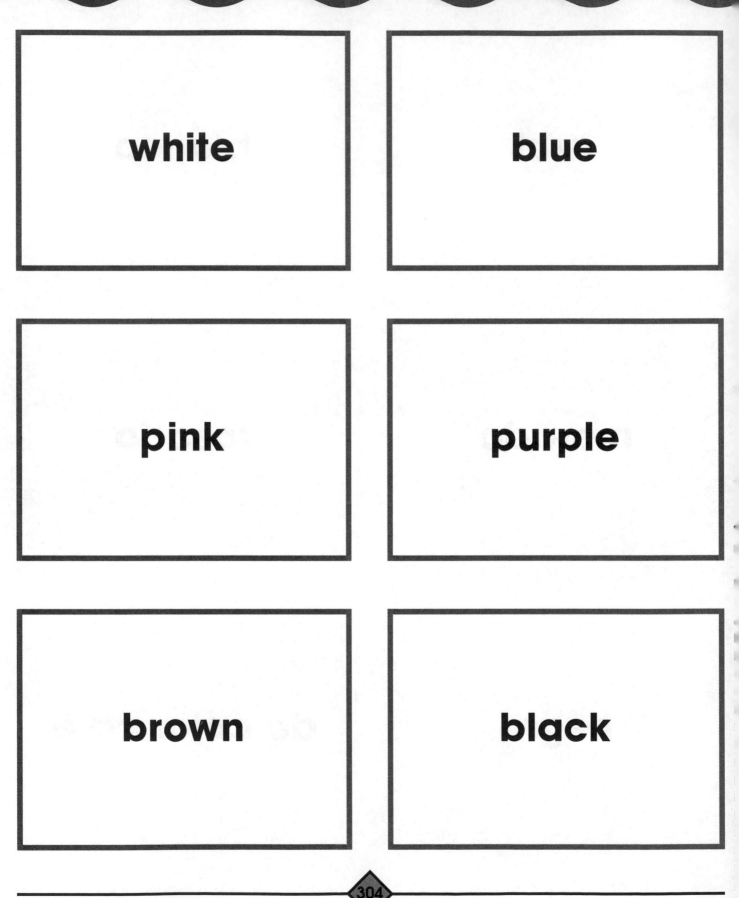

white

blue

pink

purple

brown

black

The Complete Book of Spanish

la camisa

el suéter

los pantalones

la chaqueta

el vestido

los zapatos

sweater

shirt

jacket

pants

shoes

dress

los calcetines

la falda

el gorro

los guantes

las botas

el cinturón

Nombre_____

skirt

socks

gloves

cap

belt

boots

Nombre_____

la escuela

la clase

el maestro

los alumnos

la maestra

el libro

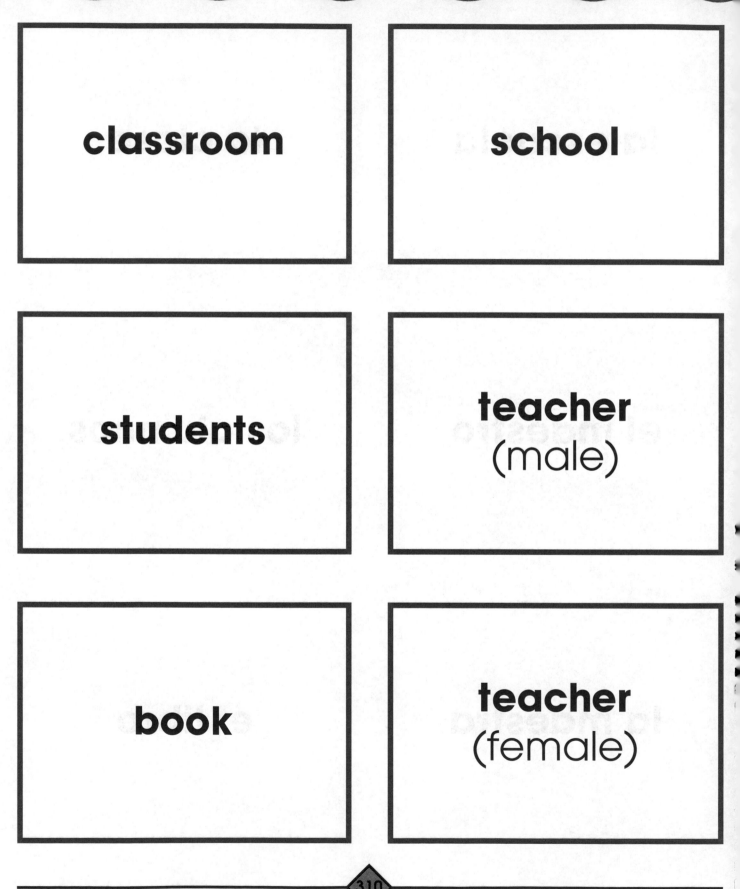

classroom

school

students

teacher
(male)

book

teacher
(female)

el lápiz

el cuaderno

el papel

las tijeras

el borrador

la pluma

notebook

pencil

scissors

paper

pen

eraser

la salida

el escritorio

el reloj

la mochila

la silla

la regla

Nombre_____

desk

exit

backpack

clock

ruler

chair

el crayón

la escritura

la lectura

el inglés

las matemáticas

las ciencias

handwriting

crayon

English

reading

science

math

Nombre_____

las ciencias sociales

el rectángulo

el círculo

el triángulo

el cuadrado

el diamante

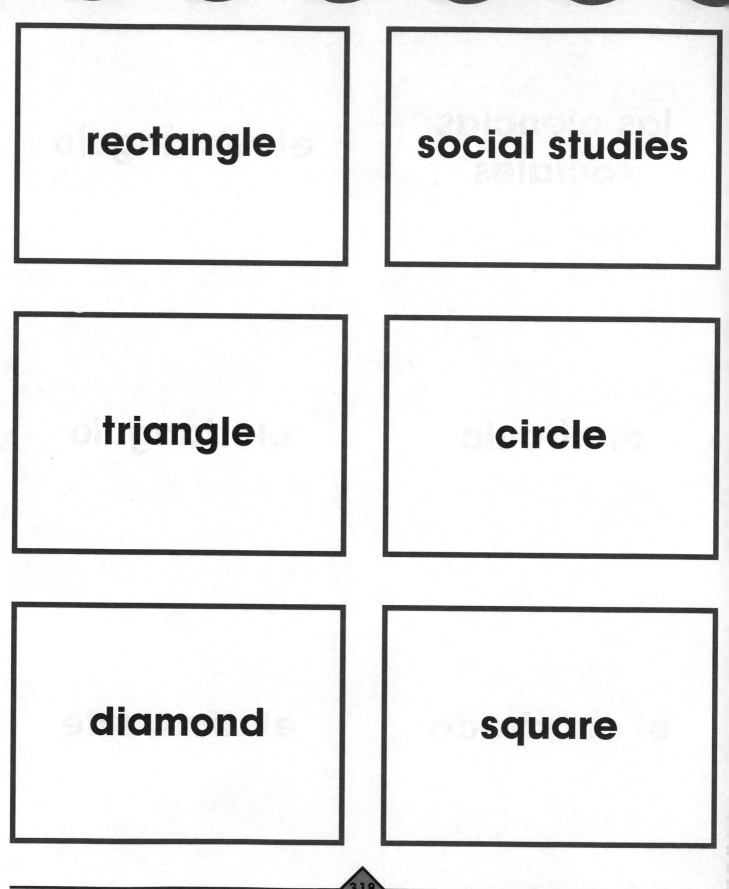

rectangle

social studies

triangle

circle

diamond

square

Nombre_____

Final Review

tú

lean

tres

¡Hola!

madre

queso

cuaderno

rosado

camisa

ojos

gato

feo

escuela

The Complete Book of Spanish

Final Review

For each English word given, write the Spanish word with the same meaning. Use the number of blanks as clues. Can you find the hidden word spelled down in each list?

four ___ ___ | ___ ___ ___

hand ___ ___ ___

blue ___ ___ ___

fruit ___ | ___ ___ ___

chair ___ | ___ ___ ___

church ___ | ___ ___ ___ ___

hello ___ ___ | ___

boots ___ ___ | ___ ___ ___

mother ___ ___ | ___ ___

kitchen ___ ___ | ___ ___ ___ ___

clean ___ ___ | ___ ___ ___

thirty ___ ___ ___ | ___ ___ ___

paint ___ ___ | ___ ___ ___

friend (m) ___ ___ | ___ ___ ___

to eat ___ ___ | ___ ___

the letter h ___ ___ | ___ ___

Saturday ___ ___ ___ | ___ ___

horse ___ ___ ___ ___ | ___ ___

milk ___ ___ ___ | ___ ___

black ___ ___ | ___ ___

you (formal) ___ ___ | ___ ___

goodbye ___ ___ | ___ ___ ___

store ___ ___ ___ | ___ ___

teacher (female) ___ ___ ___ | ___ ___ ___

hat ___ | ___ ___ ___ ___ ___

Hidden Words

1. _____

2. _____

3. _____

Handwriting Practice

After each lesson, use handwriting practice to reinforce the new vocabulary. The vocabulary is organized by lesson. Write the Spanish words from the recent (or past) lesson on the lines provided on pages 323 and 324.

Vocabulary Organized by Lesson

Numbers

cero
uno
dos
tres
cuatro
cinco
seis
siete
ocho
nueve
diez
once
doce
trece
catorce
quince
dieciséis
diecisiete
dieciocho
diecinueve
veinte
veintiuno
veintidós
veintitrés
veinticuatro
veinticinco

veintiséis
veintisiete
veintiocho
veintinueve
treinta

Colors

rojo
azul
verde
anaranjado
morado
amarillo
café
negro
blanco
rosado

Basic Expressions

Me llamo
¿Cómo estás?
Estoy bien.
Estoy mal.
Estoy así así.
¿Cuántos años tienes?
Tengo _____ años.

hola
amigo
amiga
sí
no
por favor
gracias
¡Hasta luego!
adiós
maestro
maestra
señor
señora
señorita
¡Buenos días!
¡Buenas tardes!
¡Buenas noches!
Vamos a contar.

Days of the Week

lunes
martes
miércoles
jueves
viernes
sábado
domingo

hoy
ayer
mañana

Classroom Objects

silla
mesa
tijeras
libro
lápiz
borrador
ventana
puerta
papel
cuaderno
escritorio
pluma

Clothing

falda
cinturón
chaqueta
calcetines
camisa
vestido
sombrero
pantalones

Handwriting Practice

guantes
botas
zapatos
pantalones cortos

Food

ensalada
plátano
manzana
papa
pan
naranja
queso
carne
sopa
fruta
jugo
vegetales
sandwich
leche
agua
pollo

Community

escuela
iglesia
casa
biblioteca
tienda
parque
museo
apartamento

cine
granja
restaurante
zoológico

The Body

cuerpo
cabeza
mano
pierna
hombro
brazo
dedo
pie
rodilla
estómago
cara
ojos
orejas
pelo
boca
nariz
dientes

The Family

hermano
hija
hermana
padre
tío
primos
abuelo

familia
abuela
hijo
madre
tía

Animals

gato
perro
pájaro
pez
pato
oso
rana
caballo
vaca
abeja

The House

casa
cocina
sala
dormitorio
cama
cuchara
lámpara
sofá

Adjectives

alegre
nuevo
pequeño

feo
limpio
sucio
bonita
triste
viejo
grande

Commands

corten
peguen
pinten
canten
abran
cierren
levántense
siéntense
párense
dibujen

Verbs

comer
beber
dormir
tocar
hablar
limpiar
mirar
dar

Handwriting Practice

Handwriting Practice

_____

_____

_____

_____

_____

_____

_____

_____

_____

_____

_____

_____

_____

_____

Glossary

abeja	bee	*casa*	house
abran	open	*catorce*	fourteen
abrigo	coat	*cero*	zero
abuela	grandmother	*chaqueta*	jacket
abuelo	grandfather	*cierren*	close
adiós	goodbye	*cinco*	five
agua	water	*cine*	movie theater
alegre	happy	*cinturón*	belt
amarillo	yellow	*ciudad*	city
amiga	friend (f)	*cocina*	kitchen
amigo	friend (m)	*comer*	to eat
anaranjado	orange	*contar*	to count
años	years	*corten*	cut
apartamento	apartment	*cuaderno*	notebook
así así	so-so	*cuatro*	four
ayer	yesterday	*cuchara*	spoon
azul	blue	*cuerpo*	body
beber	drink	*dar*	to give
biblioteca	library	*dedo*	finger/toe
bien	well/fine	*día*	day
blanco	white	*dibujen*	draw
blusa	blouse	*diecinueve*	nineteen
boca	mouth	*dieciocho*	eighteen
bonito	pretty	*dieciséis*	sixteen
borrador	eraser	*diecisiete*	seventeen
botas	boots	*dientes*	teeth
brazo	arm	*diez*	ten
caballo	horse	*doce*	twelve
cabeza	head	*domingo*	Sunday
café	brown	*dormir*	to sleep
calcetines	socks	*dormitorio*	bedroom
cama	bed	*dos*	two
camisa	shirt	*ensalada*	salad
canten	sing	*escritorio*	desk
cara	face	*escuela*	school
carne	meat	*estoy*	I am

Glossary

estómago	stomach	*martes*	Tuesday
falda	skirt	*Me llamo*	My name is
familia	family	*mesa*	table
feo	ugly	*miércoles*	Wednesday
fruta	fruit	*mirar*	to look at
gato	cat	*morado*	purple
gracias	thank you	*museo*	museum
grande	big	*naranja*	orange
granja	farm	*nariz*	nose
guantes	gloves	*negro*	black
hablar	to speak	*no*	no
hermana	sister	*noches*	night
hermano	brother	*nueve*	nine
hija	daughter	*nuevo*	new
hijo	son	*ocho*	eight
hola	hello	*ojos*	eyes
hombro	shoulder	*once*	eleven
hoy	today	*orejas*	ears
iglesia	church	*oso*	bear
jueves	Thursday	*padre*	father
jugo	juice	*pájaro*	bird
lámpara	lamp	*pan*	bread
lápiz	pencil	*pantalones*	pants
leche	milk	*pantalones cortos*	shorts
levántense	stand up	*papa*	potato
libro	book	*papel*	paper
limpiar	to clean	*parque*	park
limpio	clean	*pato*	duck
lunes	Monday	*párense*	stop
madre	mother	*peguen*	glue
maestra	teacher (f)	*pelo*	hair
maestro	teacher (m)	*pequeño*	small
mal	bad, not well	*perro*	dog
mano	hand	*pez*	fish
manzana	apple	*pie*	foot
mañana	tomorrow	*pierna*	leg

The Complete Book of Spanish

Glossary

pinten	paint	tío	uncle
plátano	banana	tocar	to touch
pluma	pen	trece	thirteen
pollo	chicken	treinta	thirty
por favor	please	tres	three
primos	cousins	triste	sad
puerta	door	uno	one
queso	cheese	vaca	cow
quince	fifteen	Vamos a contar.	Let's count.
rana	frog	vegetales	vegetables
restaurante	restaurant	veinte	twenty
rodilla	knee	veinticinco	twenty-five
rojo	red	veinticuatro	twenty-four
rosado	pink	veintidós	twenty-two
sala	room	veintinueve	twenty-nine
sandalias	sandals	veintiocho	twenty-eight
sandwich	sandwich	veintiséis	twenty-six
sábado	Saturday	veintisiete	twenty-seven
scis	six	veintitrés	twenty-three
señor	Mr.	veintiuno	twenty-one
señora	Mrs.	ventana	window
señorita	Miss	verde	green
siete	seven	vestido	dress
siéntense	sit down	viejo	old
silla	chair	viernes	Friday
sí	yes	zapatos	shoes
sofá	couch	zoológico	zoo
sombrero	hat	¿Cómo estás?	How are you? (familiar)
sopa	soup		
sucio	dirty	¿Cuántos años tienes?	How old are you? (familiar)
tardes	afternoon		
Tengo ___ años.	I am __ years old.	¡Buenas noches!	Good night!
tienda	store	¡Buenas tardes!	Good afternoon!
tienes	you are	¡Buenos días!	Good morning!
tijeras	scissors	¡Hasta luego!	See you later!
tía	aunt		

The Complete Book of Spanish

Bibliography of Children's Literature

Your child will enjoy listening to stories in Spanish. There are many excellent and familiar children's books available in Spanish. The books have beautiful art that engages your child and assists in comprehension. The bibliography is organized to help you choose the books related to the topics taught in *The Complete Book of Spanish*. Whenever possible, read the book first in Spanish and then in English.

Reading out loud to your child in Spanish will stretch them intellectually. Although much of the vocabulary may be unfamiliar, your child will be able to follow the basic story line in Spanish. Your child will gain exposure to the language as they listen to a familiar story, look at the pictures, and strain to catch words they may know.

Before you read, discuss the story. Turn the pages and ask your child to predict what the story might be about. Encourage your child to name pictured items in Spanish. Activate prior knowledge by discussing your child's experiences with the book's topic. When your child is engaged, begin reading.

As you read in Spanish, stop periodically to check for understanding. Ask brief questions about the actions of the characters. Acknowledge your child's predictions as they occur in the story. Quickly explain things that you think your child might have missed. Keep the rhythm of the story as much as you can. Keep your comprehension checks brief so you do not lose your child's attention.

After reading, discuss the story and conduct activities related to the book topic. Ask questions that require your child to think back to the story line or reread passages. Ask your child to explain why an event happened in the story. Review vocabulary that is familiar to your child. Read the book out loud several times. Allow your child to choose the book during independent reading time.

As you reread a book, ask your child to read out loud with you. This works especially well in stories that have repetition or predictable passages. Practice the lines in Spanish that you want your child to read out loud.

Most importantly, have fun with your child. Celebrate the joy of reading in a new language. Listen to the beauty of the language and enjoy the pictures.

Bibliography of Children's Literature

Name of Book	Author	Language	Related Topics
A la cama	Moira Kemp Mathew Price	Spanish	animals
Azulín visita a México	Virginia Poulet	Spanish	Mexico
Buenas noches, luna Goodnight, Moon	Margaret Wise Brown	Spanish English	house, general
¿Cuántos son?	Maribel Suárez	Spanish	numbers
Cuenta con Gato Galano	Donald Charles	Spanish	numbers
El Conejo Andarín The Runaway Bunny	Margaret Wise Brown	Spanish English	animals, family, general
El tesoro de Azulín	Virginia Poulet	Spanish	adjectives
Gordito, Gordón, Gato Galano	Donald Charles	Spanish	food
Huevos verdes con jamón Green Eggs and Ham	Dr. Seuss	Spanish English	food, general
Los gatitos The Kitten Book	Jan Pflogg	Spanish English	animals
¿Has visto a mi patito?	Nancy Tafuri	Spanish	animals

Bibliography of Children's Literature

Name of Book	Author	Language	Related Topics
La primera Navidad de Clifford / *Clifford's First Christmas*	Norman Bridwell	Spanish English	Christmas
La ropa	Moira Kemp Mathew Price	Spanish	clothes, animals
La semilla de zanahoria	Ruth Krauss	Spanish	food (carrot), general vocabulary
Let's Eat	Hideo Shirotani	bilingual	food
Los colores	Maribel Suárez	Spanish	colors
Mi primera visita al zoo	J. M. Parramón G. Sales	Spanish	animals
Mis primeros colores	Isidro Sánchez	Spanish	colors
Mis primeros números	Isidro Sánchez	Spanish	numbers
Osos, osos, aquí y allí	Rita Milios	Spanish	animals (bears)
Perro grande, perro pequeño / *Big Dog, Little Dog*	P. D. Eastman	bilingual	adjectives, general vocabulary
¿Qué color? / *What Color?*	Hideo Shirotani	bilingual	colors

Bibliography of Children's Literature

Name of Book	Author	Language	Related Topics
¿Quién es la bestia?	Keith Baker	Spanish	animals
Salí de paseo	Sue Williams	Spanish	animals
Say Hola to Spanish	Susan Middleton Elya	bilingual	introduction to the language
Se venden gorras / Hats for Sale	Esphyr Slobodkina	Spanish English	clothing, animals, general
Somos un arco iris	Nancy María Grande Tabor	bilingual	cultural awareness
Esta casa está hecha de lodo / This House Is Made of Mud	Ken Buchanan	bilingual	house, general
Too Many Tamales	Gary Soto	English	cultural awareness
Un día feliz	Ruth Krauss	Spanish	animals
Un murmullo es silencioso	Carolyn Lunn	Spanish	adjectives, general vocabulary
Yo soy	Rita Milios	Spanish	self-adjectives, general vocabulary

Answer Key

Page 8

Numbers Review

Write the number next to the Spanish word. Circle the correct number of animals for each number shown. Then, color the pictures.

uno	1
cinco	5
dos	2
cuatro	4
tres	3

Colors Will Vary.

Page 9

Matching Numbers

Draw a line from the word to the correct picture. Then, color the pictures.

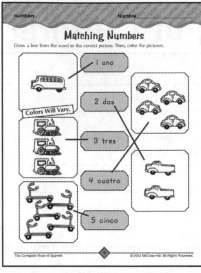

1 uno
2 dos
3 tres
4 cuatro
5 cinco

Colors Will Vary.

Page 10

Number the Stars

Draw the correct number of stars next to each number.

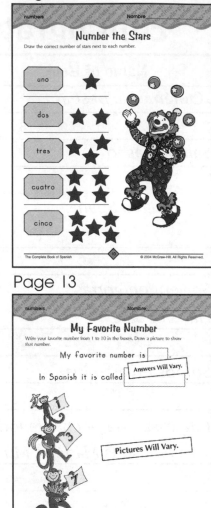

uno
dos
tres
cuatro
cinco

Page 11

1–10 Matching

Draw a line to match each object to the number that is written in Spanish.

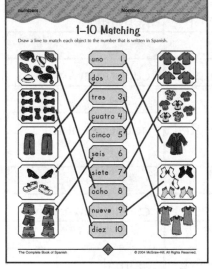

uno	1
dos	2
tres	3
cuatro	4
cinco	5
seis	6
siete	7
ocho	8
nueve	9
diez	10

Page 12

Count the Cookies

In each box at the left, write the number that matches the Spanish word. Cross out the correct number of cookies to show the number written in Spanish. The first one is done for you.

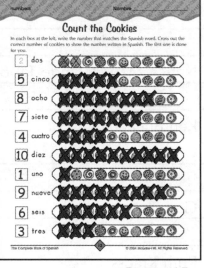

2	dos
5	cinco
8	ocho
7	siete
4	cuatro
10	diez
1	uno
9	nueve
6	seis
3	tres

Page 13

My Favorite Number

Write your favorite number from 1 to 10 in the boxes. Draw a picture to show that number.

My favorite number is

In Spanish it is called

Answers Will Vary.

Pictures Will Vary.

Page 14

Circles 1–10

Draw the correct number of circles in each box.

uno		seis	
dos		siete	
tres		ocho	
cuatro		nueve	
cinco		diez	

Page 15

Coloring 0–10

Color or circle the number of butterflies that shows the number written in Spanish.

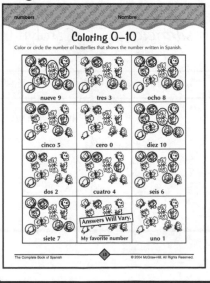

nueve 9	tres 3	ocho 8
cinco 5	cero 0	diez 10
dos 2	cuatro 4	seis 6
siete 7	My favorite number	uno 1

Answers Will Vary.

Page 16

Numbers 0–10

Trace, then write each of the number words from 0 to 10 in Spanish. Use the words at the left to help you.

0	cero	cero	cero	cero	cero
1	uno	uno	uno	uno	uno
2	dos	dos	dos	dos	dos
3	tres	tres	tres	tres	tres
4	cuatro	cuatro	cuatro	cuatro
5	cinco	cinco	cinco	cinco	cinco
6	seis	seis	seis	seis	seis
7	siete	siete	siete	siete	siete
8	ocho	ocho	ocho	ocho	ocho
9	nueve	nueve	nueve	nueve
10	diez	diez	diez	diez	diez

Page 17

Numbers 0–10

Say each word out loud. Circle the number that tells the meaning of the word.

seis	5	0	(6)
ocho	1	9	(8)
uno	3	(1)	8
cero	8	10	(0)
siete	9	(7)	1
tres	0	(3)	5
diez	(10)	8	7
nueve	4	2	(9)
cuatro	7	5	(4)
dos	(2)	6	3
cinco	6	4	(5)

Page 18

Dot-to-Dot

Connect the dots. Start with the Spanish word for one and stop at ten. What shape did you get? __STAR__

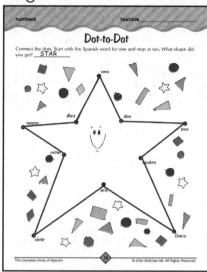

Page 19

Numbers 0–20

In the left column, write the number words from 0 to 10 in Spanish. Use the words in the box below to help you. Then, in the second column, write the numbers beside each Spanish word. Examples are done for you.

0	cero		
1	uno	11	once
2	dos	12	doce
3	tres	13	trece
4	cuatro	14	catorce
5	cinco	15	quince
6	seis	16	dieciséis
7	siete	17	diecisiete
8	ocho	18	dieciocho
9	nueve	19	diecinueve
10	diez	20	veinte

siete ocho uno seis nueve
cero cinco dos cuatro diez tres

Now, count from 1 to 20 in Spanish. Point to the numbers as you say them.

Page 20

Show Your Numbers

In each box, write the number for the word written. Then, draw and color pictures that show the numbers.

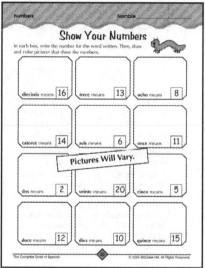

dieciséis means 16	trece means 13	ocho means 8
catorce means 14	seis means 6	once means 11
dos means 2	veinte means 20	cinco means 5
doce means 12	diez means 10	quince means 15

Pictures Will Vary.

Page 21

Sunshine 0–20

Write the number for each Spanish word. Cross out the correct number of suns to show the number written in Spanish. The first is done for you.

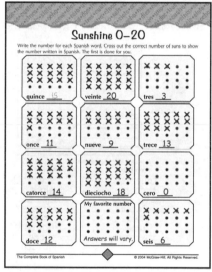

quince 15	veinte 20	tres 3
once 11	nueve 9	trece 13
catorce 14	dieciocho 18	cero 0
doce 12	My favorite number — Answers will vary.	seis 6

Page 22

Numbers Crossword

Use the words at the bottom to help you with this crossword puzzle. Write the Spanish number words in the puzzle spaces. Follow the English clues.

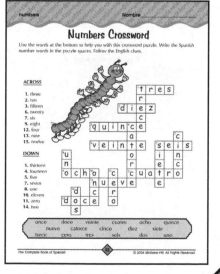

ACROSS
1. three
2. ten
3. fifteen
6. twenty
7. six
9. eight
12. four
13. nine
15. twelve

DOWN
1. thirteen
4. fourteen
5. five
7. seven
8. one
10. eleven
11. zero
14. two

once doce veinte cuatro ocho quince
nueve catorce tres cinco diez siete
trece cero. tres seis dos uno

Page 23

Numbers

After each numeral, write the number word in Spanish. Refer to the words below to help you.

Word Bank

veinte	cuatro	nueve	diez	diecisiete	quince
doce	once	trece	siete	uno	tres
catorce	dos	cero	ocho	cinco	dieciséis
diecinueve		dieciocho		seis	

0	cero	11	once
1	uno	12	doce
2	dos	13	trece
3	tres	14	catorce
4	cuatro	15	quince
5	cinco	16	dieciséis
6	seis	17	diecisiete
7	siete	18	dieciocho
8	ocho	19	diecinueve
9	nueve	20	veinte
10	diez		

Page 24

Numbers Illustration

Write the number. Draw that many things in the box. The first one is done for you.

☆☆☆☆ ☆☆☆☆		
ocho means __8__	cinco means __5__	diecisiete means __17__
doce means __12__	uno means __1__	dos means __2__
Pictures Will Vary.		
catorce means __14__	nueve means __9__	veinte means __20__
siete means __7__	cuatro means __4__	quince means __15__

Page 25

Number Puzzle

Write the English number words in the puzzle spaces. Follow the Spanish clues.

Word Bank
one, two, six, eight, nine, ten, eleven, thirteen, fourteen, seventeen, eighteen, twenty

Puzzle answers: eight, twenty, seven, six, four[teen], nine, eight, two, thirteen, eleven

Down
1. diecisiete
2. veinte
4. uno
8. nueve
9. dieciocho
10. diez

Across
1. seis
3. ocho
5. catorce
6. trece
7. once
10. dos

Page 26

Counting On

Follow a pattern to write the numbers from 21–29. Change veinte (20) to veinti and add the number words from uno to nueve. (Watch for accent marks on dos, tres, and seis.)

Rewrite the number words in the Word Bank in order.

Word Bank
veintiséis, veinticinco, treinta, veintiocho, veintidós, veintiuno, veintinueve, veinticuatro, veintisiete, veintitrés

21	veintiuno	26	veintiséis
22	veintidós	27	veintisiete
23	veintitrés	28	veintiocho
24	veinticuatro	29	veintinueve
25	veinticinco	30	treinta

Complete the pattern to write the numbers from 31–39. Use the word y to join treinta (30) with the number words uno to nueve.

30	treinta	35	treinta y cinco
31	treinta y uno	36	treinta y seis
32	treinta y dos	37	treinta y siete
33	treinta y tres	38	treinta y ocho
34	treinta y cuatro	39	treinta y nueve

Page 27

Number Find

Circle the Spanish number words that you find in the word search. Then write the English meaning of each word.

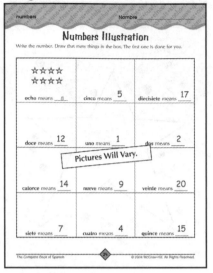

Spanish Word	English	Spanish Word	English
doce	twelve	treinta	thirty
catorce	fourteen	siete	seven
veintiuno	twenty-one	ocho	eight
veintisiete	twenty-seven	veintidós	twenty-two
once	eleven	cinco	five
dos	two	seis	six
nueve	nine	quince	fifteen
veinte	twenty	tres	three
		dieciocho	eighteen

Page 28

Counting by Tens

The Spanish numbers ten, twenty, thirty, forty, and fifty are written out of order below. Write the value of each number word in the blank.

__30__ treinta   __50__ cincuenta   __40__ cuarenta
__10__ diez   __20__ veinte

Write the numbers from 30–59 in Spanish.

30	treinta	45	cuarenta y cinco
31	treinta y uno	46	cuarenta y seis
32	treinta y dos	47	cuarenta y siete
33	treinta y tres	48	cuarenta y ocho
34	treinta y cuatro	49	cuarenta y nueve
35	treinta y cinco	50	cincuenta
36	treinta y seis	51	cincuenta y uno
37	treinta y siete	52	cincuenta y dos
38	treinta y ocho	53	cincuenta y tres
39	treinta y nueve	54	cincuenta y cuatro
40	cuarenta	55	cincuenta y cinco
41	cuarenta y uno	56	cincuenta y seis
42	cuarenta y dos	57	cincuenta y siete
43	cuarenta y tres	58	cincuenta y ocho
44	cuarenta y cuatro	59	cincuenta y nueve

Page 29

Number Search

Circle the Spanish number words that you find in the word search. Write the English meanings at the bottom of the page next to the Spanish words from the puzzle.

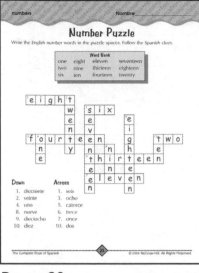

Spanish Word	English	Spanish Word	English
cero	zero	dos	two
cuatro	four	seis	six
ocho	eight	diez	ten
doce	twelve	catorce	fourteen
veinte	twenty	cuarenta	forty
uno	one	tres	three
cinco	five	siete	seven
nueve	nine	once	eleven
trece	thirteen	quince	fifteen
treinta	thirty	cincuenta	fifty

Page 31

Listening Practice

Say the Spanish word for each number out loud. Write the first letter of the words you hear.

1. u   4. c   7. s
2. d   5. c   8. o
3. t   6. s   9. n

Color the letters of the Spanish alphabet. Say them in Spanish as you color them.

A B C D E F G
H I J K L M N
Ñ O P Q R S T
U V W X Y Z

Page 32

The Alphabet

El abecedario (the alphabet)

a	a	h	hache	ñ	eñe	u	u
b	be	i	i	o	o	v	ve
c	ce	j	jota	p	pe	w	doble u
ch	che	k	ka	q	cu	x	equis
d	de	l	ele	r	ere	y	i griega
e	e	ll	elle	rr	ese	z	zeta
f	efe	m	eme	t	te		
g	ge	n	ene				

Listening Practice

Write each letter of the alphabet as you say it out loud.

1. a   7. f   13. l   19. p   25. v
2. b   8. g   14. ll   20. q   26. w
3. c   9. h   15. m   21. r   27. x
4. ch   10. i   16. n   22. s   28. y
5. d   11. j   17. ñ   23. t   29. z
6. e   12. k   18. o   24. u

Page 33

The Alphabet

El abecedario (the alphabet)

a	a	k	ka	s	ese
b	be	l	ele	t	te
c	ce	ll	elle	u	u
d	de	m	eme	v	ve
e	e	n	ene	w	doble ve
f	efe	ñ	eñe	x	equis
g	ge	o	o	y	i griega
h	hache	p	pe	z	zeta
i	i	q	cu		
j	jota	r	ere		

Listening Practice

Write the Spanish word for each number below. Then, spell each word out loud.

1. uno
2. dos
3. tres
4. cuatro
5. cinco
6. seis
7. siete
8. ocho
9. nueve
10. diez
11. once
12. doce
13. trece
14. catorce
15. quince
16. dieciséis

Page 36

Using You

Spanish uses two different forms of the pronoun you.

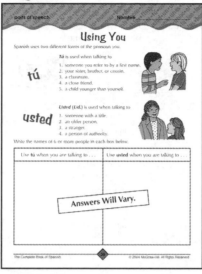

Tú is used when talking to
1. someone you refer to by a first name.
2. your sister, brother, or cousin.
3. a classmate.
4. a close friend.
5. a child younger than yourself.

Usted (Ud.) is used when talking to
1. someone with a title.
2. an older person.
3. a stranger.
4. a person of authority.

Write the names of 6 or more people in each box below.

Use **tú** when you are talking to . . .	Use **usted** when you are talking to . . .
Answers Will Vary.	

Page 37

Picking Pronouns

Spanish uses two different forms of the pronoun you.

Tú is used when talking to
1. someone you refer to by a first name.
2. your sister, brother, or cousin.
3. a classmate.
4. a close friend.
5. a child younger than yourself.

Usted (Ud.) is used when talking to
1. someone with a title.
2. an older person.
3. a stranger.
4. a person of authority.

Explain to whom you might be talking and what you are asking in each question.

¿Cuál es tu nombre? **Asking someone your own age or younger what his/her name is.**

¿Cómo se llama usted? **Asking someone older or a person of authority what his/her name is.**

¿Cómo estás tú? **Asking someone your own age or younger how he/she is.**

¿Cómo está usted? **Asking someone older or a person of authority how he/she is.**

¿Cuántos años tienes tú? **Asking someone your own age or younger how old he/she is.**

¿Cuántos años tiene usted? **Asking someone older or a person with authority how old he/she is.**

Page 38

Who Is It?

Write the names of people you may know that fit each description below.

tú–informal or familiar form of you	
someone you refer to by first name	
your sister or brother (or cousin)	
a classmate	Answers Will Vary.
a close friend	
a child younger than yourself	

usted–formal or polite form of you	
someone with a title	
an older person	Answers Will Vary.
a stranger	
a person of authority	

How would you speak to each person below? Write tú or usted after each person named.

1. Dr. Hackett — usted
2. Susana — tú
3. a four-year-old — tú
4. your grandfather — usted
5. the governor — usted
6. your best friend — tú
7. your sister — tú
8. the principal — usted
9. a classmate — tú
10. a stranger — usted

Page 39

Masculine and Feminine

All Spanish nouns and adjectives have gender. This means they are either masculine or feminine. Here are two basic rules to help determine the gender of words. There are other rules for gender which you will learn as you study more Spanish.

1. Spanish words ending in *o* are usually masculine.
2. Spanish words ending in *a* are usually feminine.

Write the following words in the charts to determine their gender. Write the English meanings to the right. Use a Spanish-English dictionary if you need help.

maestra, libro, escritorio, negro, abrigo, sopa, tienda
amigo, ventana, pluma, museo, vestido, fruta, museo
silla, puerta, anaranjado, amiga, camisa, queso, casa
rojo, cuaderno, blanco, falda, chaqueta

Masculine		**Feminine**	
words ending in o	meaning of the word	words ending in a	meaning of the word
amigo	friend (male)	maestra	teacher (female)
rojo	red	silla	chair
libro	book	ventana	window
cuaderno	notebook	puerta	door
escritorio	desk	pluma	pen
anaranjado	orange	amiga	friend (female)
museo	museum	falda	skirt
blanco	white	camisa	shirt
negro	black	chaqueta	jacket
maestro	teacher (male)	sopa	soup
abrigo	coat	fruta	fruit
vestido	dress	tienda	store
queso	cheese	casa	house

Page 40

More Than One

Spanish nouns can be placed into two groups–singular (one of something) or plural (more than one of something). Nouns that end in *-s* are usually plural. Nouns ending in other letters are usually singular.

Read the following familiar nouns. Write S if the noun is singular and P if the noun is plural.

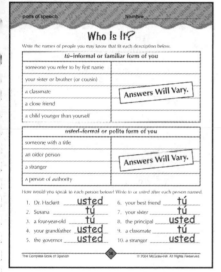

1. calcetines — P
2. dedo — S
3. botas — P
4. cuerpo — S
5. vegetales — P
6. ciudad — S
7. escuela — S
8. sandalias — P
9. zapatos — S
10. guantes — P
11. casa — S
12. boca — S

Follow these rules to write the following Spanish words in the plural.

1. If the word ends in a vowel, add *-s*.
2. If the word ends in a consonant, add *-es*.
3. If the word ends in z, change the z to c before adding *-es*.

1. carne — carnes
2. silla — sillas
3. ciudad — ciudades
4. lápiz — lápices
5. azul — azules
6. nariz — narices
7. abrigo — abrigos
8. señor — señores
9. borrador — borradores
10. pollo — pollos

Page 41

More and More

Write the plural form of each Spanish clue word in the puzzle.

h o m b r o s
f a l d a s
z a p a t o s
m u s e o s
n a r i c e s
g a t o s   s o m b r e r o s
o s o s
l á p i c e s

Across
1. hombro
4. falda
5. zapato
7. museo
8. nariz
10. gato
11. sombrero
13. oso
14. lápiz

Down
2. borrador
3. vaso
6. escuela
9. casa
12. mesa

Page 42

It's a Small World

In Spanish, there are four ways to say "the"–*el, la, los,* and *las*. The definite article (the) agrees with its noun in gender (masculine or feminine) and number (singular or plural). Masculine singular nouns go with el. Feminine singular nouns go with la.

Examples: el libro (the book) el papel (the paper)
la silla (the chair) la regla (the ruler)

Masculine plural nouns go with los. Feminine plural nouns go with las.

Examples: los libros (the books) los papeles (the papers)
las sillas (the chairs) las reglas (the rulers)

Refer to the Word Bank to complete the chart. Write the singular and plural forms and the correct definite articles. The first ones have been done for you.

Word Bank: cuaderno, mesa, pluma, oso, falda, papel, gato, bota, silla, libro

English	Masculine Singular	Masculine Plural
the book	el libro	los libros
the paper	el papel	los papeles
the notebook	el cuaderno	los cuadernos
the cat	el gato	los gatos
the bear	el oso	los osos

English	Feminine Singular	Feminine Plural
the chair	la silla	las sillas
the table	la mesa	las mesas
the boot	la bota	las botas
the skirt	la falda	las faldas
the pen	la pluma	las plumas

Page 43

parts of speech   Nombre _____

One or Some

In English, the words *a*, *an*, and *some* are indefinite articles. In Spanish, there are four indefinite articles—un, una, unos, and unas.

Masculine singular nouns go with *un*. Feminine singular nouns go with *una*.

Examples: un libro (a book)   una silla (a chair)
            un papel (a paper)   una mesa (a table)

Masculine plural nouns go with *unos*. Feminine plural nouns go with *unas*.

Examples: unos libros (some books)   unas sillas (some chairs)
            unos papeles (some papers)   unas mesas (some tables)

Refer to the Word Bank to complete the chart. Write the singular and plural forms and the correct indefinite articles. The first one has been done for you.

| Word Bank | cuaderno | mesa | pluma | oso | falda |
| | papel | gato | bota | silla | libro |

English	Masculine Singular	Masculine Plural
a book	un libro	unos libros
a paper	un papel	unos papeles
a notebook	un cuaderno	unos cuadernos
a cat	un gato	unos gatos
a bear	un oso	unos osos

English	Feminine Singular	Feminine Plural
a chair	una silla	unas sillas
a table	una mesa	unas mesas
a boot	una bota	unas botas
a skirt	una falda	unas faldas
a pen	una pluma	unas plumas

The Complete Book of Spanish   © 2004 McGraw-Hill. All Rights Reserved.

Page 44

parts of speech   Nombre _____

Watch How Many

Refer to the given articles and nouns to translate the following phrases into Spanish. Use a Spanish-English dictionary if you need help.

Articles			
un	una	unos	unas
el	la	los	las

Nouns			
cine (m)	dedo	elefantes (m)	museo	tijeras
cara	cuerpo	borradores (m)	agua	cuadernos
blusa	falda	cucharas	boca	caballos
				camas

1. a skirt   una falda
2. the body   el cuerpo
3. the spoons   las cucharas
4. the mouth   la boca
5. the elephants los elefantes
6. some scissors unas tijeras
7. the finger   el dedo
8. a museum   un museo
9. the face   la cara
10. a blouse   una blusa
11. the horses   los caballos
12. some notebooks unos cuadernos
13. the beds   las camas
14. a movie theater un cine

The Complete Book of Spanish   © 2004 McGraw-Hill. All Rights Reserved.

Page 45

parts of speech   Nombre _____

Pretty Colors

Adjectives are words that tell about or describe nouns. Color each box as indicated in Spanish. Use a Spanish-English dictionary if you need help.

rojo	azul	verde	anaranjado	morado
amarillo	café	negro	blanco	rosado

Here are some new adjectives. Copy the Spanish words in the boxes. Write the Spanish words next to the English at the bottom of the page.

bonita	bonita		feo	feo	
grande	grande		pequeño	pequeño	
limpio	limpio		sucio	sucio	
viejo	viejo		nuevo	nuevo	
alegre	alegre		triste	triste	

old   viejo   pretty bonita   sad   triste
big   grande   small   pequeño   happy alegre
new   nuevo   dirty   sucio   ugly feo
clean limpio

The Complete Book of Spanish   © 2004 McGraw-Hill. All Rights Reserved.

Page 46

parts of speech   Nombre _____

Abundant Adjectives

Circle the Spanish words you find in the word search. Then, write the English meanings next to the Spanish words at the bottom of the page.

rojo _____ red   de color café brown   azul _____ blue
limpio _____ clean   feo _____ ugly   sucio _____ dirty
pequeño _____ small   viejo _____ old   negro _____ black
amarillo _____ yellow   anaranjado orange   triste _____ sad
grande _____ large   blanco _____ white   rosado _____ pink
morado _____ purple   nuevo _____ new   verde _____ green
alegre _____ happy   bonito _____ pretty

The Complete Book of Spanish   © 2004 McGraw-Hill. All Rights Reserved.

Page 47

parts of speech   Nombre _____

Words to Describe

Descriptive adjectives are words that describe nouns. Refer to the Word Bank to write the Spanish adjective that describes each picture.

Word Bank					
alegre	grande	nuevo	pequeño	feo	rico
limpio	sucio	bonita	triste	viejo	pobre
alto	bajo	abierto	cerrado		

large	new	ugly	happy
grande	nuevo	feo	alegre

old	sad	small	clean
viejo	triste	pequeño	limpio

pretty	dirty	tall	open
bonita	sucio	alto	abierto

rich	short	closed	poor
rico	bajo	cerrado	pobre

The Complete Book of Spanish   © 2004 McGraw-Hill. All Rights Reserved.

Page 48

parts of speech   Nombre _____

Words to Describe

Write the Spanish words for the clue words in the crossword puzzle.

Across
3. poor
7. open
9. tall
11. clean
12. dirty
13. new

Down
1. ugly
2. closed
4. happy
5. pretty
6. large
8. old
10. sad

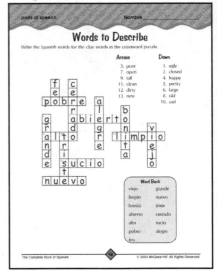

Word Bank	
viejo	grande
limpio	nuevo
bonita	triste
abierto	cerrado
alto	sucio
pobre	alegre
feo	

The Complete Book of Spanish   © 2004 McGraw-Hill. All Rights Reserved.

Page 49

parts of speech   Nombre _____

Open and Close

Would you know what to do if your teacher told you to do something in Spanish? In each box, copy the Spanish word. Then, write the English word below it from the Word Bank.

corten	cierren
corten	cierren
cut	close
peguen	levántense
peguen	levántense
glue	stand up
pinten	siéntense
pinten	siéntense
paint	sit down
canten	párense
canten	párense
sing	stop
abran	dibujen
abran	dibujen
open	draw

Word Bank				
sing	sit down	close	glue	open
stop	cut	paint	stand up	draw

The Complete Book of Spanish   © 2004 McGraw-Hill. All Rights Reserved.

Page 50

parts of speech   Nombre _____

Write It Down

Write the Spanish word for each clue in the crossword puzzle.

Across
3. paint
4. open
7. stand up
8. sing
9. paste
10. cut

Down
1. draw
2. sit down
5. close
6. stop

Word Bank		
canten	corten	levántense
párense	cierren	abran
siéntense	pinten	dibujen
	peguen	

The Complete Book of Spanish   © 2004 McGraw-Hill. All Rights Reserved.

Answer Key

Page 52

parts of speech Nombre

Simon Says

Would you know what to do if your teacher asked you to do something in Spanish? In each box, copy the Spanish word then write the English meaning below it.

siéntense	abran	peguen
sit down	open	glue

levántense	pinten	corten
stand up	paint	cut

cierren	caminen	corran
close	walk	run

escriban	escuchen	lean
write	listen	read

Word Bank

sit down	glue	paint	close	run	listen
open	stand up	cut	walk	write	read

The Complete Book of Spanish — © 2004 McGraw-Hill. All Rights Reserved.

Page 53

parts of speech Nombre

Search and Find

Circle the Spanish words you find in the word search. Write the English meanings at the bottom of the page next to the Spanish words from the puzzle.

Spanish Word	English	Spanish Word	English
corten	cut	corran	run
levántense	stand up	escriban	write
peguen	glue	abran	open
siéntense	sit down	escuchen	listen
caminen	walk	cierren	close
pinten	paint	lean	read

The Complete Book of Spanish — © 2004 McGraw-Hill. All Rights Reserved.

Page 54

parts of speech Nombre

Action Words

In each box, copy the Spanish action verbs. Then, write the English word below it.

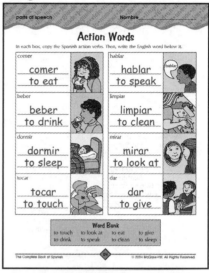

comer	hablar
to eat	to speak

beber	limpiar
to drink	to clean

dormir	mirar
to sleep	to look at

tocar	dar
to touch	to give

Word Bank

to touch	to look at	to eat	to give
to drink	to speak	to clean	to sleep

The Complete Book of Spanish — © 2004 McGraw-Hill. All Rights Reserved.

Page 55

parts of speech Nombre

Action Figures

Write the Spanish words from the Word Bank that fit in these word blocks. Write the English below the blocks.

Word Bank

mirar	limpiar	tocar	beber
hablar	comer	dar	dormir

1. c o m e r — to eat
2. b e b e r — to drink
3. m i r a r — to look at
4. d a r — to give
5. l i m p i a r — to clean
6. h a b l a r — to speak
7. d o r m i r — to sleep
8. t o c a r — to touch

English

to eat	to look at	to speak	to touch
to clean	to sleep	to drink	to give

The Complete Book of Spanish — © 2004 McGraw-Hill. All Rights Reserved.

Page 56

parts of speech Nombre

First Sentences

Create original sentences in Spanish using these sentence starters and the verbs in the Word Bank. You may use one sentence starter more than once. Write the English meanings on the lines below the Spanish.

Word Bank

comer	beber	dormir	tocar
hablar	limpiar	mirar	dar

Sentence Starters

Me gusta _____	(I like _____.)
No me gusta _____	(I don't like _____.)
Quiero _____	(I want _____.)
Necesito _____	(I need _____.)

1.
2.
3. **Sentences Will Vary.**
4.
5.

The Complete Book of Spanish — © 2004 McGraw-Hill. All Rights Reserved.

Page 57

parts of speech Nombre

Action Words

Refer to the Word Bank to write the Spanish word that matches each picture.

Word Bank	comer	estudiar	limpiar	mirar	jugar	dar
	hablar	beber	dormir	trabajar	tocar	ir

limpiar	tocar	comer
hablar	mirar	beber
dar	dormir	estudiar
ir	trabajar	jugar

The Complete Book of Spanish — © 2004 McGraw-Hill. All Rights Reserved.

Page 58

parts of speech Nombre

Reading and Writing

Circle the Spanish words that you find in the word search. Write the English meanings at the bottom of the page next to the Spanish words from the puzzle.

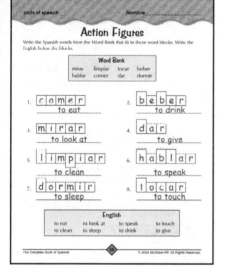

Spanish Word	English	Spanish Word	English
comer	to eat	jugar	to play
hablar	to speak	dormir	to sleep
estudiar	to study	mirar	to look
beber	to drink	trabajar	to work
limpiar	to clean	tocar	to touch
ir	to go	dar	to give

The Complete Book of Spanish — © 2004 McGraw-Hill. All Rights Reserved.

Page 59

parts of speech Nombre

Capitals

Spanish uses capital letters less often than the English language. Follow these rules as your guide.

Capitalization Rules

1. All Spanish sentences begin with capital letters.
2. Names of people begin with capital letters.
3. Names of places (cities, regions, countries, continents) and holidays begin with capital letters.
4. Titles are not capitalized unless abbreviated (señor—Sr., usted—Ud.).
5. Some words that are normally capitalized in English may not be capitalized in Spanish (nationalities, religions, languages, months, and days).

Write sí if the word should be capitalized. Write no if it should remain lowercase.

1. sarah — sí
2. inglés — no
3. navidad — sí
4. español — no
5. mexicano — no
6. áfrica — sí
7. señor — no
8. enero — no
9. domingo — no
10. católico — no
11. santa fé — sí
12. viernes — no
13. méxico — sí
14. julio — no
15. colorado — sí
16. miguel — sí

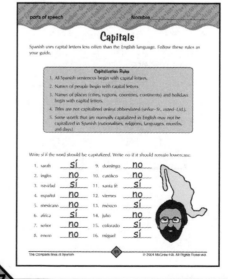

The Complete Book of Spanish — © 2004 McGraw-Hill. All Rights Reserved.

The Complete Book of Spanish

Page 60

Categories

Read the list of words given. Write the words in the proper columns. If the word needs a capital letter, write it that way.

los angeles · españa · ustedes · americano · lunes
maria · susana · san antonio · américa del norte · méxico
uds. · sr. · santa fé · español · católico
inglés · sra. · oceano pacifico · señora · señor
san diego · viernes · juan · josé
señorita · cuba · septiembre · mexicano

People	Place	Titles	Not Capitalized
María	Los Angeles	Uds.	inglés
Susana	San Diego	Sr.	señorita
Juan	España	Sra.	viernes
José	Cuba		ustedes
	San Antonio		septiembre
	Sante Fé		americano
	Océano Pacifico		español
	América del Norte		señora
	México		mexicano
			lunes
			católico
			señor

Page 64

Pictures of Greetings

Say the greeting out loud. Circle the picture that tells the meaning of each word.

¡Hola!
¿Cómo te llamas?
Me llamo...
¿Cómo estás?
bien
mal
así, así
¡Adiós!

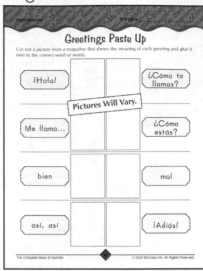

Page 65

Greetings Paste Up

Cut out a picture from a magazine that shows the meaning of each greeting and glue it next to the correct word or words.

¡Hola!   ¿Cómo te llamas?
Me llamo...   ¿Cómo estás?
bien   mal
así, así   ¡Adiós!

Pictures Will Vary.

Page 67

Introductions Review

Say each expression out loud. Circle the picture that tells the meaning of each word.

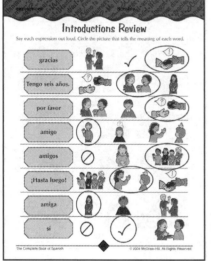

gracias
Tengo seis años.
por favor
amigo
amigos
¡Hasta luego!
amiga
sí

Page 68

What's Your Name?

Word Bank
I'm so-so.   What's your name?   I'm well/fine.
I'm ____ years old.   I'm not doing well.   My name is ____.
I'm not well.   How are you?   How old are you?

Refer to the Word Bank to translate the Spanish questions and answers into English.

1. ¿Cómo te llamas? **What is your name?**
   Me llamo ____. **My name is ____.**
2. ¿Cómo estás? **How are you?**
   Estoy bien/mal/así así. **I'm fine. I'm not well. I'm so-so.**
3. ¿Cuántos años tienes? **How old are you?**
   Tengo ____ años. **I am ____ years old.**

Word Bank
hello   please   friend   yes
no   thank you   goodbye   See you later!

Write the English meaning after the Spanish word.

4. hola **hello**
5. amigo, amiga **friend (m/f)**
6. sí **yes**
7. no **no**
8. por favor **please**
9. gracias **thank you**
10. ¡Hasta luego! **See you later!**
11. adiós **goodbye**

Page 69

Word Blocks

Write the Spanish words from the Word Bank that fit in these word blocks. Don't forget the punctuation. Write the English meanings below the blocks.

1. h o l a — hello
2. p o r f a v o r — please
3. n o — no   ¡H a s t a l u e g o! — See you later!
5. ¿C ó m o e s t á s? — How are you?
6. ¿C ó m o t e l l a m a s? — What is your name?
7. a d i ó s — goodbye

Spanish Word Bank
por favor   adiós   Estoy bien.
hola   ¡Hasta luego!   ¿Cómo te llamas?
no   ¿Cómo estás?

8. E s t o y b i e n. — I am fine.

Page 70

Greetings

Write the English meaning of the Spanish words and phrases.

1. señor — **Mr.**
2. señora — **Mrs.**
3. señorita — **Miss**
4. maestro — **teacher (male)**
5. maestra — **teacher (female)**
6. ¡Buenos días! — **Good morning!**
7. ¡Buenas tardes! — **Good afternoon!**
8. ¡Buenas noches! — **Good night!**
9. Vamos a contar. — **Let's count.**

Word Bank
Mr.   Good night!   Good morning!
Good afternoon!   teacher (female)   teacher (male)
Miss   Let's count.   Mrs.

Draw a picture to show the time of day that you use each expression.

Pictures Will Vary.

¡Buenos días!   ¡Buenas tardes!   ¡Buenas noches!

Page 71

Spanish Greetings

Write the Spanish word for each clue in the crossword puzzle.

Across
1. bad
4. good
7. teacher (male)
9. friend (female)
10. Mr.
11. Miss

Down
2. friend (male)
3. hello
5. thank you
6. goodbye
7. teacher (female)
8. Mrs.

Word Bank
amiga   mal
señora   señor
maestra   bien
adiós   hola
señorita   gracias
amigo   maestro

Answer Key

Page 72

Greetings

Refer to the Word Bank to translate the Spanish greetings, questions, and answers.

¡Buenos días! **Good morning!**
¡Buenas tardes! **Good afternoon!**
¡Buenas noches! **Good night!**
¿Cómo estás? **How are you?**
bien, gracias **fine, thank you**
mal **not well**
así así **ok/so-so**
¿Cómo te llamas? **What is your name?**
Me llamo **My name is**
¿Cuántos años tienes? **How old are you?**
Tengo _____ años. **I am _____ years old.**
adiós **goodbye** hola **hello**

Word Bank
goodbye
Good morning!
I am _____ years old.
fine, thank you
Good afternoon!
hello
How old are you?
How are you?
What is your name?
My name is
not well
ok/so-so
Good night!

Word Bank
teacher (m/f)   Miss   no
Mr.   friend (m/f)   please
Mrs.   yes

Refer to the Word Bank to translate the Spanish vocabulary.

amigo/amiga **friend (m/f)**
sí **yes** no **no** por favor **please**
señor **Mr.** señora **Mrs.**
maestro/maestra **teacher (m/f)**
señorita **Miss**

Page 73

Find the Words

Circle the Spanish words that you find in the word search. Write the English meanings at the bottom of the page next to the Spanish words from the puzzle.

Spanish Word	English	Spanish Word	English
amigo	friend (m)	adiós	goodbye
gracias	thank you	maestro	teacher (m)
mal	not well	señor	Mr.
amiga	friend (f)	bien	fine
hola	hello	maestra	teacher (f)
no	no	señora	Mrs.
señorita	Miss	sí	yes

Page 76

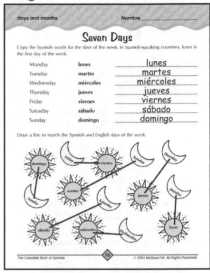

Seven Days

Copy the Spanish words for the days of the week. In Spanish-speaking countries, *lunes* is the first day of the week.

Monday	lunes	lunes
Tuesday	martes	martes
Wednesday	miércoles	miércoles
Thursday	jueves	jueves
Friday	viernes	viernes
Saturday	sábado	sábado
Sunday	domingo	domingo

Draw a line to match the Spanish and English days of the week.

Page 77

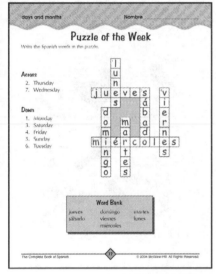

Puzzle of the Week

Write the Spanish words in the puzzle.

Across
2. Thursday
7. Wednesday

Down
1. Monday
3. Saturday
4. Friday
5. Sunday
6. Tuesday

Word Bank
jueves   domingo   martes
sábado   viernes   lunes
miércoles

Page 79

Yesterday and Today

Write the Spanish words for the days of the week. Remember: in Spanish-speaking countries, Monday is the first day of the week.

Word Bank
miércoles   jueves   sábado
viernes   lunes   martes
domingo

Monday	lunes
Tuesday	martes
Wednesday	miércoles
Thursday	jueves
Friday	viernes
Saturday	sábado
Sunday	domingo

If today is Monday, yesterday was Sunday. Complete the following chart by identifying the missing days in Spanish. The first one is done for you.

ayer (yesterday)	hoy (today)	mañana (tomorrow)
martes	miércoles	jueves
lunes	martes	miércoles
jueves	viernes	sábado
sábado	domingo	lunes
miércoles	jueves	viernes
domingo	lunes	martes
viernes	sábado	domingo

Page 80

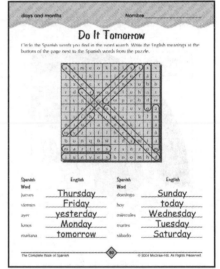

Do It Tomorrow

Circle the Spanish words you find in the word search. Write the English meanings at the bottom of the page next to the Spanish words from the puzzle.

Spanish Word	English	Spanish Word	English
jueves	Thursday	domingo	Sunday
viernes	Friday	hoy	today
ayer	yesterday	miércoles	Wednesday
lunes	Monday	martes	Tuesday
mañana	tomorrow	sábado	Saturday

Page 81

Rain in April

Refer to the Word Bank to write the Spanish word for the given month. Then, in the box, draw a picture of something that happens in that month of the year. Remember that Spanish months do not begin with capital letters.

Word Bank
agosto   septiembre   noviembre   mayo
junio   enero   octubre   febrero
marzo   julio   diciembre   abril

January	enero	Pictures Will Vary.	July	julio	Pictures Will Vary.
February	febrero		August	agosto	
March	marzo		September	septiembre	
April	abril		October	octubre	
May	mayo		November	noviembre	
June	junio		December	diciembre	

Page 82

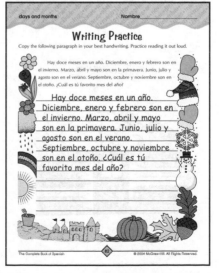

Writing Practice

Copy the following paragraph in your best handwriting. Practice reading it out loud.

Hay doce meses en un año. Diciembre, enero y febrero son en el invierno. Marzo, abril y mayo son en la primavera. Junio, julio y agosto son en el verano. Septiembre, octubre y noviembre son en el otoño. ¿Cuál es tú favorito mes del año?

Hay doce meses en un año. Diciembre, enero y febrero son en el invierno. Marzo, abril y mayo son en la primavera. Junio, julio y agosto son en el verano. Septiembre, octubre y noviembre son en el otoño. ¿Cuál es tú favorito mes del año?

Answer Key

Page 83

Page 86
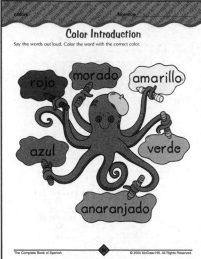

Page 87

Page 88

Page 89
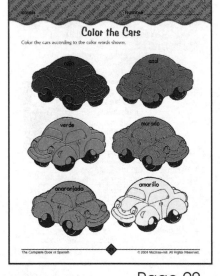

Page 90
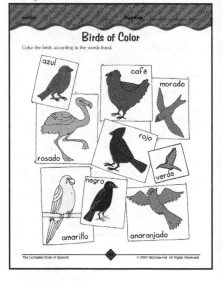

Page 91
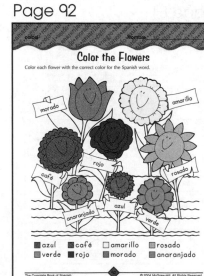

Page 92

The Complete Book of Spanish

Answer Key

Page 93

Color Search

Cut out pictures from a magazine that match the colors below. Glue each picture next to the correct color word.

rojo	Pictures Will Vary.	amarillo	Pictures Will Vary.
azul		café	
verde		negro	
anaranjado		blanco	
morado		rosado	

Page 94

Moving Colors

Color the pictures according to the words listed.

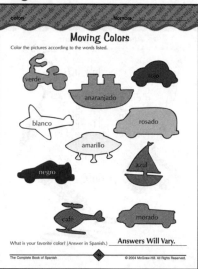

verde, rojo, anaranjado, blanco, rosado, amarillo, negro, azul, café, morado

What is your favorite color? (Answer in Spanish.) **Answers Will Vary.**

Page 95

Color Away

Write the English word below the Spanish color listed. Use the words at the bottom to help you. Color the pictures using that color.

rojo means	anaranjado means	café means
red	orange	brown
azul means	morado means	blanco means
blue	purple	white
verde means	amarillo means	rosado means
green	yellow	pink

Which color was not used? __negro (black)__

| white | red | orange | green | pink |
| blue | purple | yellow | brown | black |

Page 96

Color Crossword

Write the correct Spanish color words in the spaces. Follow the English color clues.

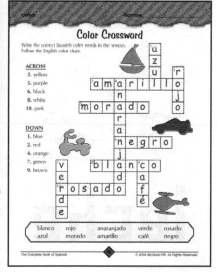

ACROSS
3. yellow
5. purple
6. black
8. white
10. pink

DOWN
1. blue
2. red
4. orange
7. green
9. brown

Crossword answers: azul, amarillo, rojo, morado, negro, naranja, verde, blanco, rosado, café

| blanco | rojo | anaranjado | verde | rosado |
| azul | morado | amarillo | café | negro |

Page 97

Color Copy

Copy the following words in the color of each word. Which word is hard to see with the actual color? __blanco (white)__

rojo	rojo
azul	azul
verde	verde
anaranjado	anaranjado
morado	morado
amarillo	amarillo
café	café
negro	negro
blanco	blanco
rosado	rosado

Page 98

Colorful Flowers

Color the flowers according to the Spanish color words shown below.

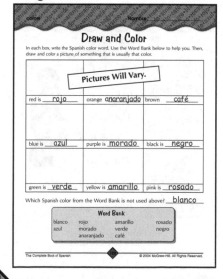

Page 99

Color Find

Circle the Spanish color words that you find in the wordsearch. Then, write the English meaning of each word.

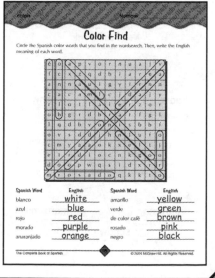

Spanish Word	English	Spanish Word	English
blanco	white	amarillo	yellow
azul	blue	verde	green
rojo	red	de color café	brown
morado	purple	rosado	pink
anaranjado	orange	negro	black

Page 100

Draw and Color

In each box, write the Spanish color word. Use the Word Bank below to help you. Then, draw and color a picture of something that is usually that color.

Pictures Will Vary.

red is __rojo__	orange __anaranjado__	brown __café__
blue is __azul__	purple is __morado__	black is __negro__
green is __verde__	yellow is __amarillo__	pink is __rosado__

Which Spanish color from the Word Bank is not used above? __blanco__

Word Bank

blanco	rojo	amarillo	rosado
azul	morado	verde	negro
	anaranjado	café	

The Complete Book of Spanish

Answer Key

Page 101

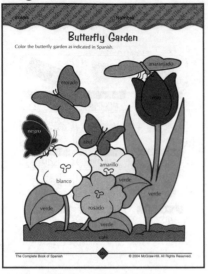

Butterfly Garden

Color the butterfly garden as indicated in Spanish.

Page 102

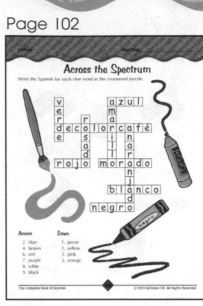

Across the Spectrum

Write the Spanish for each clue word in the crossword puzzle.

Across
2. blue
4. brown
6. red
7. purple
8. white
9. black

Down
1. green
2. yellow
3. pink
5. orange

Page 106

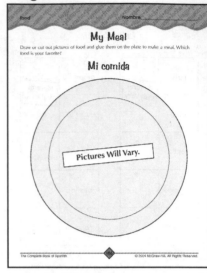

My Meal

Draw or cut out pictures of food and glue them on the plate to make a meal. Which food is your favorite?

Mi comida

Pictures Will Vary.

Page 107

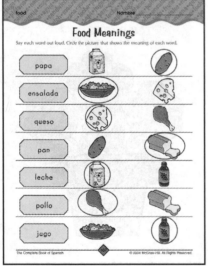

Food Meanings

Say each word out loud. Circle the picture that shows the meaning of each word.

papa
ensalada
queso
pan
leche
pollo
jugo

Page 108

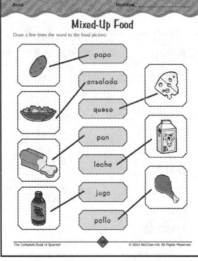

Mixed-Up Food

Draw a line from the word to the food picture.

papa
ensalada
queso
pan
leche
jugo
pollo

Page 109

Food Words

Say each word out loud. Write the English word next to it.

queso — cheese
leche — milk
papa — potato
jugo — juice
pan — bread
pollo — chicken
ensalada — salad
leche

Color the blocks with letters.
Do not color the blocks with numbers. What word did you find?

leche

Page 110

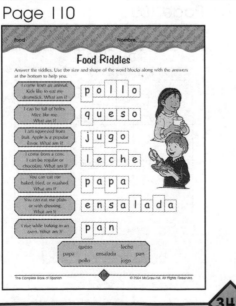

Food Riddles

Answer the riddles. Use the size and shape of the word blocks along with the answers at the bottom to help you.

I come from an animal. Kids like to eat me drumstick. What am I? — p o l l o

I can be full of holes. Mice like me. What am I? — q u e s o

I am squeezed from fruit. Apple is a popular flavor. What am I? — j u g o

I come from a cow. I can be regular or chocolate. What am I? — l e c h e

You can eat me baked, fried, or mashed. What am I? — p a p a

You can eat me plain or with dressing. What am I? — e n s a l a d a

I rise while baking in an oven. What am I? — p a n

queso   leche
papa   ensalada   pan
pollo   jugo

Page 111

New Food Words

Say each word out loud. Copy each word and color the picture.

sopa — sopa
agua — agua
naranja — naranja
carne — carne
Colors Will Vary.
plátano — plátano
sandwich — sandwich
manzana — manzana

Answer Key

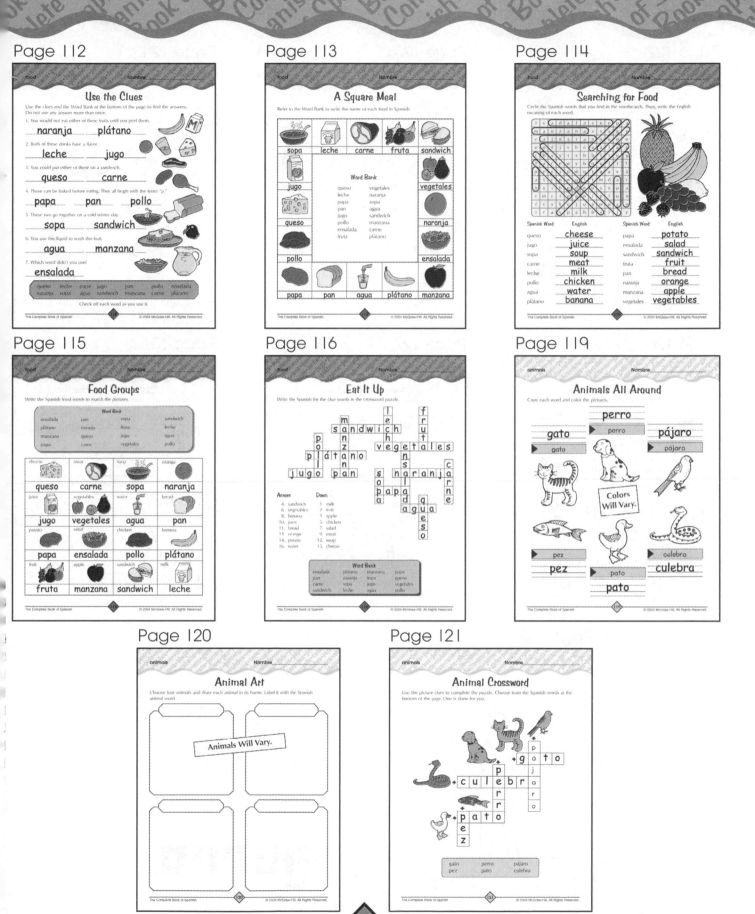

Page 112

Use the Clues

Use the clues and the Word Bank at the bottom of the page to find the answers. Do not use any answer more than once.

1. You would not eat either of these fruits until you peel them.
naranja   plátano

2. Both of these drinks have a flavor.
leche   jugo

3. You could put either of these on a sandwich.
queso   carne

4. These can be baked before eating. They all begin with the letter "p."
papa   pan   pollo

5. These two go together on a cold winter day.
sopa   sandwich

6. You use this liquid to wash this fruit.
agua   manzana

7. Which word didn't you use?
ensalada

queso leche papa jugo pan pollo ensalada
naranja sopa agua sandwich manzana carne plátano

Check off each word as you use it.

Page 113

A Square Meal

Refer to the Word Bank to write the name of each food in Spanish.

sopa | leche | carne | fruta | sandwich
jugo | | | | vegetales
queso | | | | naranja
pollo | | | | ensalada
papa | pan | agua | plátano | manzana

Word Bank
queso vegetales
leche naranja
papa sopa
pan agua
jugo sandwich
pollo manzana
ensalada carne
fruta plátano

Page 114

Searching for Food

Circle the Spanish words that you find in the wordsearch. Then, write the English meaning of each word.

Spanish Word	English	Spanish Word	English
queso	cheese	papa	potato
jugo	juice	ensalada	salad
sopa	soup	sandwich	sandwich
carne	meat	fruta	fruit
leche	milk	pan	bread
pollo	chicken	naranja	orange
agua	water	manzana	apple
plátano	banana	vegetales	vegetables

Page 115

Food Groups

Write the Spanish food words to match the pictures.

Word Bank
ensalada pan sopa sandwich
plátano naranja fruta leche
manzana queso jugo agua
papa carne vegetales pollo

cheese	meat	soup	orange
queso	carne	sopa	naranja
juice	vegetables	water	bread
jugo	vegetales	agua	pan
potato	salad	chicken	banana
papa	ensalada	pollo	plátano
fruit	apple	sandwich	milk
fruta	manzana	sandwich	leche

Page 116

Eat It Up

Write the Spanish for the clue words in the crossword puzzle.

Across
4. sandwich
6. vegetables
8. banana
10. juice
11. bread
13. orange
14. potato
16. water

Down
1. milk
2. fruit
3. apple
5. chicken
7. salad
9. meat
12. soup
15. cheese

Word Bank
ensalada plátano manzana papa
pan naranja fruta queso
carne sopa jugo vegetales
sandwich leche agua pollo

Page 119

Animals All Around

Copy each word and color the pictures.

gato → gato
perro → perro
pájaro → pájaro

Colors Will Vary.

pez → pez
pato → pato
culebra → culebra

Page 120

Animal Art

Choose four animals and draw each animal in its home. Label it with the Spanish animal word.

Animals Will Vary.

Page 121

Animal Crossword

Use the picture clues to complete the puzzle. Choose from the Spanish words at the bottom of the page. One is done for you.

gato
perro
pájaro
culebra
pez
pato

gato perro pájaro
pez pato culebra

Answer Key

Page 122

animals Nombre _____

Use the Clues

Answer the questions. Use the clues and the Spanish words at the bottom of the page. You may use answers more than once.

1. Both words begin with the same letter, and both animals have feathers.
   __pájaro__ __pato__

2. These two animals walk and are house pets.
   __gato__ __perro__

3. Both animals begin with the same letter. One quacks and the other barks.
   __perro__ __pato__

4. Both of these animals like to live in the water.
   __pato__ __pez__

5. These animals do not have fur or feathers.
   __culebra__ __pez__

6. The first animal likes to chase and catch the second animal. They both end with the letter o.
   __gato__ __pájaro__
   (or perro/gato)

| gato | perro | pájaro |
| pez | pato | culebra |

The Complete Book of Spanish · 122 · © 2004 McGraw-Hill. All Rights Reserved.

Page 123

animals Nombre _____

Pet Parade

In each box, copy the name of each animal in Spanish. Write the Spanish words next to the English words at the bottom of the page.

pájaro	pájaro (bird)	caballo	caballo (horse)
perro	perro (dog)	oso	oso (bear)
rana	rana (frog)	gato	gato (cat)
vaca	vaca (cow)	pato	pato (duck)
abeja	abeja (bee)	pez	pez (fish)

Write the Spanish words from above next to the English words.

cat __gato__   cow __vaca__   duck __pato__
dog __perro__   horse __caballo__   frog __rana__
bird __pájaro__   bear __oso__   bee __abeja__
fish __pez__

The Complete Book of Spanish · 123 · © 2004 McGraw-Hill. All Rights Reserved.

Page 124

animals Nombre _____

Three Little Kittens

Draw a picture to match the Spanish phrase in each box.

seis pájaros	cuatro perros
nueve abejas	siete osos
tres gatos	dos vacas
cinco patos	ocho caballos
diez ranas	un pez

The Complete Book of Spanish · 124 · © 2004 McGraw-Hill. All Rights Reserved.

Page 126

animals Nombre _____

Animal Match

Copy the Spanish word under each picture.

oso	rana	caballo	vaca
__oso__	__rana__	__caballo__	__vaca__
elefante	oveja	puerco	gallina
__elefante__	__oveja__	__puerco__	__gallina__
gato	tortuga	mariposa	dinosaurio
__gato__	__tortuga__	__mariposa__	__dinosaurio__

Write the Spanish for each animal name.

1. butterfly __mariposa__   7. cow __vaca__
2. sheep __oveja__   8. bear __oso__
3. cat __gato__   9. elephant __elefante__
4. dinosaur __dinosaurio__   10. horse __caballo__
5. chicken __gallina__   11. turtle __tortuga__
6. pig __puerco__   12. frog __rana__

The Complete Book of Spanish · 126 · © 2004 McGraw-Hill. All Rights Reserved.

Page 127

animals Nombre _____

Rainbow Roundup

Copy the following Spanish sentences on the lines provided. Then, write the English meanings.

1. El oso es blanco. __El oso es blanco.__
   __The bear is white.__

2. El puerco es rosado. __El puerco es rosado.__
   __The pig is pink.__

3. La rana es roja. __La rana es roja.__
   __The frog is red.__

4. La tortuga es verde. __La tortuga es verde.__
   __The turtle is green.__

5. El dinosaurio es azul. __El dinosaurio es azul.__
   __The dinosaur is blue.__

6. El gato es anaranjado. __El gato es anaranjado.__
   __The cat is orange.__

7. La gallina es amarilla. __La gallina es amarilla.__
   __The chicken is yellow.__

8. El caballo es de color café. __El caballo es de color café.__
   __The horse is brown.__

9. La mariposa es morada. __La mariposa es morada.__
   __The butterfly is purple.__

The Complete Book of Spanish · 127 · © 2004 McGraw-Hill. All Rights Reserved.

Page 131

clothes Nombre _____

Clothing Match-Ups

Draw a line from the word to match the correct picture. Color the picture.

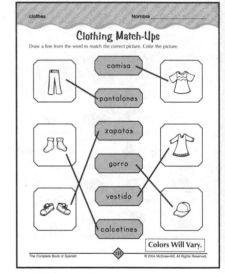

camisa
pantalones
zapatos
gorro
vestido
calcetines

Colors Will Vary.

The Complete Book of Spanish · 131 · © 2004 McGraw-Hill. All Rights Reserved.

Page 132

clothes Nombre _____

How Are You?

Draw or cut out pictures of clothes to make a boy or girl. Write the names of the clothes next to them in Spanish.

Who are you?

Pictures Will Vary.

How are you?   What are you wearing?

The Complete Book of Spanish · 132 · © 2004 McGraw-Hill. All Rights Reserved.

Page 133

clothes Nombre _____

Clothes to Color

Cut out pictures and glue them next to the correct words.

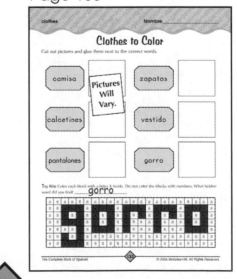

camisa	Pictures Will Vary.	zapatos	
calcetines		vestido	
pantalones		gorro	

Try this: Color each block with a letter X inside. Do not color the blocks with numbers. What hidden word did you find? __gorro__

The Complete Book of Spanish · 133 · © 2004 McGraw-Hill. All Rights Reserved.

Answer Key

Page 134

Page 135

Page 136

Page 137

Page 138

Page 139
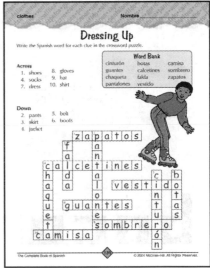

Page 140

Colorful Clothing

Copy each sentence in Spanish on the first line. Write the English meaning on the second line.

1. El vestido es rojo. **El vestido es rojo.**
   The dress is red.
2. La camisa es de color café. **La camisa es de color café.**
   The shirt is brown.
3. El sombrero es morado. **El sombrero es morado.**
   The hat is purple.
4. La falda es verde. **La falda es verde.**
   The skirt is green.
5. El vestido es rosado. **El vestido es rosado.**
   The dress is pink.
6. La chaqueta es azul. **La chaqueta es azul.**
   The jacket is blue.
7. Los calcetines son amarillos. **Los calcetines son amarillos.**
   The socks are yellow.
8. El cinturón es anaranjado. **El cinturón es anaranjado.**
   The belt is orange.
9. Las botas son blancas. **Las botas son blancas.**
   The boots are white.

Page 141

Matching Clothes

At the bottom of each picture, write the English word that matches the Spanish and the pictures. Write the Spanish words next to the English at the bottom of the page.

falda	zapatos	pantalones cortos	cinturón
skirt	shoes	shorts	belt
abrigo	calcetines	vestido	botas
coat	socks	dress	boots
guantes	pantalones	chaqueta	blusa
gloves	pants	jacket	blouse
gorro	sandalias	camisa	
cap	sandals	shirt	

1. skirt **falda**
2. belt **cinturón**
3. jacket **chaqueta**
4. socks **calcetines**
5. coat **abrigo**
6. shirt **camisa**
7. sandals **sandalias**
8. dress **vestido**
9. cap **gorro**
10. pants **pantalones**
11. gloves **guantes**
12. boots **botas**
13. shoes **zapatos**
14. blouse **blusa**
15. shorts **pantalones cortos**

345

The Complete Book of Spanish

Page 142

Clothes Closet

Circle the Spanish words that you find in the puzzle. Write the English meanings at the bottom of the page next to the Spanish words from the puzzle.

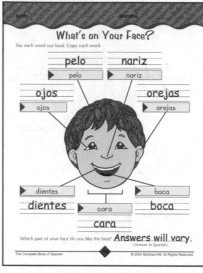

Spanish Word	English	Spanish Word	English
abrigo	coat	sandalias	sandals
guantes	gloves	calcetines	socks
blusa	blouse	falda	skirt
chaqueta	jacket	vestido	dress
pantalones	pants	camisa	shirt
botas	boots	gorro	cap
cinturón	belt	zapatos	shoes

Page 145

What's on Your Face?

Say each word out loud. Copy each word.

pelo — pelo
nariz — nariz
ojos — ojos
orejas — orejas
dientes — dientes
boca — boca
cara — cara

Which part of your face do you like the best? **Answers will vary.**
(Answer in Spanish.)

Page 146

Face Riddles

Can you guess the answers to the following riddles? Use the size and shape of the letter blocks to write the Spanish word. The answers at the bottom will help you.

There are two of me. Sometimes I need glasses. What am I?	o j o s
I like to be washed and combed. What am I?	p e l o
I help hold up glasses. When I feel an itch, I sneeze. What am I?	n a r i z
Everyone's looks a little different, in spite of the shape. What am I?	c a r a
We grow, get loose, fall out, and grow again. What are we?	d i e n t e s
"Open wide" is often said when I am too small. What am I?	b o c a
Does your mom always tell you to wash behind us? What are we?	o r e j a s

nariz   pelo   dientes
ojos   orejas   cara   boca

Page 147

A Blank Face

Fill in the blanks with the missing letters. Use the Spanish words below to help you.

nariz   pelo   dientes   ojos   orejas   cara   boca

Which word didn't you use? __cara__

Color each block that has a letter k inside. Do not color the blocks with numbers. What hidden word did you find? __boca__

Page 148

Head to Toe

Using the Word Banks, label the parts of the face and body.

nariz
ojos
orejas
dientes
pelo
cara
boca

Word Bank
cara   ojos   boca   nariz   dientes   orejas   pelo

hombro
mano
dedo
cabeza
cuerpo
estómago
brazo
pie
rodilla
dedo
pierna

Word Bank
cuerpo   cabeza   mano   pierna   hombro
brazo   dedo   pie   rodilla   estómago

Page 149

Diagonal Digits

Circle the Spanish words you find in the word search. Then write the English meanings next to the Spanish words at the bottom of the page.

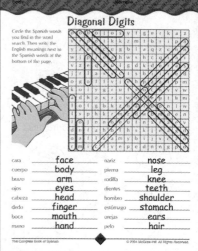

cara	face	nariz	nose
cuerpo	body	pierna	leg
brazo	arm	rodilla	knee
ojos	eyes	dientes	teeth
cabeza	head	hombro	shoulder
dedo	finger	estómago	stomach
boca	mouth	orejas	ears
mano	hand	pelo	hair

Page 150

Head and Shoulders

Refer to the Word Bank to label each body part in Spanish.

cabeza
hombro
brazo
cuerpo
estómago
mano
rodilla
pierna
pie
dedo

Word Bank
cuerpo   pie
brazo   pierna
cabeza   rodilla
dedo   hombro
mano   estómago

Page 151

Knees and Toes

Write the Spanish words for the clues in the crossword puzzle.

Word Bank
cuerpo   cabeza   mano   pierna   hombro
brazo   dedo   pie   rodilla   estómago

Across
2. foot
3. body
5. knee
6. head
7. shoulder
9. hand

Down
1. finger or toe
2. leg
4. stomach
8. arm

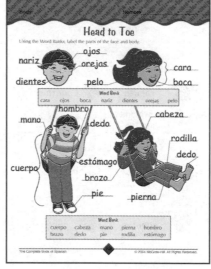

Page 152

How Are You?

Label each facial feature with a Spanish word from the Word Bank.

Word Bank
cara
ojos
boca
nariz
pelo
dientes
orejas

pelo — nariz — cara

dientes — ojos — boca — orejas

Copy the Spanish word that matches each face pictured.

alegre — triste — llorando

sonriendo — enojado — pensando

Page 153

Happy Faces

Write the Spanish for the clue words in the crossword puzzle.

Across
1. sad
3. nose
5. eyes
6. thinking
8. face
11. smiling
13. crying

Down
2. angry
4. happy
7. teeth
9. ears
10. mouth
12. hair

triste
nariz
ojos
pensando
cara
sonriendo
pelo
llorando

Word Bank

llorando	orejas	sonriendo	ojos
pelo	nariz	triste	cara
dientes	alegre	enojado	boca
pensando			

Page 157

My Family

Draw a picture of your family. Color your picture.

Mi familia

Pictures Will Vary.

Write the correct Spanish word next to each person in your picture above.

padre · hermano · abuelo
madre · hermana · abuela

Page 158

Family Word Meanings

Say each word out loud. Circle the picture that shows the meaning of each word.

padre

hermana

abuela

madre

abuelo

hermano

Page 159

Matching Family

Cut out a picture of a family out of a magazine. Glue each picture next to the correct word.

padre — hermana

Pictures Will Vary.

madre — abuelo

hermano — abuela

Try this: Color each block with a letter inside. Do not color the blocks with numbers.
What hidden word did you find? **madre**

Page 160

Family

Copy each word and color the pictures.

madre ► madre
padre ► padre

abuelo ► abuelo
abuela ► abuela

hermana ► hermana
hermano ► hermano

Colors Will Vary.

Let's learn two new words:

chico ► chico
chica ► chica

Page 161

Family Crossword

Use the Spanish words at the bottom of the page to fill in your answers.

hermana
padre — abuela
madre
chica
chico

ACROSS
1. sister
4. father
5. mother
6. girl
7. boy

DOWN
1. brother
2. grandmother
3. grandfather

padre · madre
chico · chica
abuelo · abuela
hermano · hermana

Page 162

Listen Well

Say each word out loud. Circle the picture for each Spanish word.

padre

abuelo

hermana

chica

abuela

madre

hermano

chico

Page 163

Family Ties

In each box, copy the Spanish word for family members.

la familia	la familia (family)	el hermano	el hermano (brother)
el padre	el padre (father)	la hermana	la hermana (sister)
la madre	la madre (mother)	el tío	el tío (uncle)
el hijo	el hijo (son)	la tía	la tía (aunt)
la hija	la hija (daughter)	el abuelo	el abuelo (grandfather)
los primos	los primos (cousins)	la abuela	la abuela (grandmother)

Write the Spanish words from above next to the English words.

sister la hermana family la familia father el padre
grandfather el abuelo cousins los primos mother la madre
grandmother la abuela brother el hermano daughter la hija
uncle el tío aunt la tía son el hijo

Page 164

My Family

Write the Spanish word for each clue in the crossword puzzle.

Across
2. son
3. aunt
5. sister
7. grandmother
8. brother
10. cousins

Down
1. mother
4. daughter
6. grandfather
9. uncle
10. father

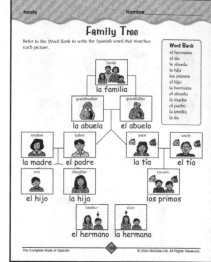

Word Bank
familia hermano hijo tía
primos madre tío abuelo
padre hermana hija abuela

Page 165

Family Tree

Refer to the Word Bank to write the Spanish word that matches each picture.

Word Bank
el hermano
el tío
la abuela
la hija
los primos
el hijo
la hermana
el abuelo
la madre
el padre
la familia
la tía

la familia
la abuela — el abuelo
la madre — el padre — la tía — el tío
el hijo — la hija — los primos
el hermano — la hermana

Page 166

Relationships

How are the following people related? Read the Spanish sentences carefully. Use the words in the Word Bank to complete each sentence. You may use each word only once, and some words may not be used at all. Then, write the English meaning of each sentence on the line below the sentence.

Word Bank
hermano hija hermana padre primos
abuela abuelo familia hijo madre tía

1. La madre de mi madre es mi **abuela**
   My mother's mother is my grandmother.

2. Los hijos de mi tío son mis **primos**
   My uncle's sons are my cousins.

3. La hija de mi madre es mi **hermana**
   My mother's daughter is my sister.

4. El hermano de mi padre es mi **tío**
   My father's brother is my uncle.

5. El padre de mi padre es mi **abuelo**
   My father's father is my grandfather.

6. El hermano de mi tío es mi **padre**
   My uncle's brother is my father.

7. La hermana de mi madre es mi **tía**
   My mother's sister is my aunt.

8. La hermana de mi tía es mi **madre**
   My aunt's sister is my mother.

Page 170

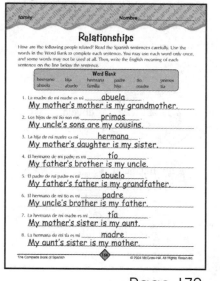

Picture This

Say each word out loud. Circle the picture that shows the meaning of each word.

casa
escuela
tienda
parque
biblioteca
museo

Page 171

My Neighborhood

Draw a picture of an imaginary neighborhood. Draw places you have learned about in this book. Add streets, trees, and whatever else you wish to make your neighborhood look nice. Color your picture.

Mi barrio

Pictures Will Vary.

Label your neighborhood with the words you learned.

casa parque biblioteca tienda escuela museo

Page 172

Places, Please

Cut out pictures that match the words below. Glue each picture next to the correct word.

casa — Pictures Will Vary. — tienda
parque — escuela
biblioteca — museo

Try this: Color each block with a letter Y inside. Do not color the blocks with numbers. What hidden word did you find? **casa**

Page 173

Places to Go

Say each word out loud. Copy each word and color the picture.

museo
escuela — museo — casa
escuela — casa
Colors Will Vary.
tienda — parque
tienda — biblioteca — parque
biblioteca

Answer Key

Page 174

A Place for Riddles

Answer the riddles. Use the size and shape of the letter blocks to write the Spanish words. The answers at the bottom of the page will help you.

Riddle	Answer
People live in me. What am I?	c a s a
If you want to buy something, you come to me. What am I?	t i e n d a
People like to come to me for playing and relaxing. What am I?	p a r q u e
I am filled with books that you can borrow. What am I?	b i b l i o t e c a
I am filled with children, desks, and books. What am I?	e s c u e l a
I often have dinosaur bones. What am I?	m u s e o

escuela   museo   casa
biblioteca   tienda   parque

Page 175

Our Town

Draw a picture of a town showing community places that you have learned. Label them in Spanish. Use the words at the bottom of the page.

Pictures Will Vary.

escuela   museo   casa
biblioteca   tienda   parque

Page 176

Place Words

Fill in the blanks for place words. Use the Spanish words at the bottom to help you.

b i b l i o t e c a
t i e n d a
m u s e o
p a r q u e
c a s a

escuela   museo   casa
biblioteca   tienda   parque

Page 177

Where Am I?

Refer to the Word Bank and write the Spanish for each place in the community pictured.

cine	museo
granja	zoológico
iglesia	biblioteca
parque	tienda
apartamento	casa
restaurante	escuela

Word Bank
escuela   granja   biblioteca   tienda
museo   casa   apartamento   zoológico
iglesia   restaurante   cine   parque

Page 178

Fitting In

Write the Spanish words from the Word Bank in these word blocks. Write the English meanings below the blocks.

Word Bank
granja   escuela   parque
cine   casa   restaurante
museo   iglesia   biblioteca
tienda

1. c a s a — house
2. g r a n j a — farm
3. m u s e o — museum
4. p a r q u e — park
5. e s c u e l a — school
6. r e s t a u r a n t e — restaurant
7. c i n e — movie theater
8. t i e n d a — store
9. i g l e s i a — church
10. b i b l i o t e c a — library

Page 180

Around the House

Copy the Spanish words. Then, write the English words below them.

casa — casa — house	sofá — sofá — couch
cocina — cocina — kitchen	cama — cama — bed
sala — sala — living room	lámpara — lámpara — lamp
dormitorio — dormitorio — bedroom	cuchara — cuchara — spoon

Word Bank
couch   kitchen   lamp   spoon
bedroom   bed   house   living room

Page 181

Around the Block

Write the Spanish words from the Word Bank that fit in these word blocks. Write the English below the blocks.

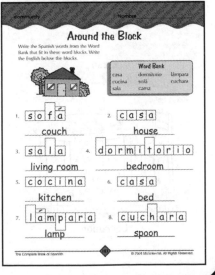

Word Bank
casa   dormitorio   lámpara
cocina   sofá   cuchara
sala   cama

1. s o f á — couch
2. c a s a — house
3. s a l a — living room
4. d o r m i t o r i o — bedroom
5. c o c i n a — kitchen
6. c a s a — bed
7. l á m p a r a — lamp
8. c u c h a r a — spoon

Page 182

A Blue House

Copy the sentences in Spanish on the first lines. Write the sentences in English on the second lines.

1. La casa es azul. La casa es azul.
   The house is blue.
2. La sala es de color café. La sala es de color café.
   The living room is brown.
3. El dormitorio es morado. El dormitorio es morado.
   The bedroom is purple.
4. La cuchara es verde. La cuchara es verde.
   The spoon is green.
5. El sofá es rosado. El sofá es rosado.
   The sofa is pink.
6. La cama es azul. La cama es azul.
   The bed is blue.
7. La lámpara es amarilla. La lámpara es amarilla.
   The lamp is yellow.

Challenge

La fruta está en la cocina. La fruta está en la cocina.
The fruit is in the kitchen.

The Complete Book of Spanish

Page 183

Around Town

Write the Spanish words to match the pictures. Write the English next to the Spanish at the bottom of the page.

park	apartment	farm	country
parque	apartamento	granja	campo
restaurant	school	city	library
restaurante	escuela	ciudad	biblioteca
museum	zoo	church	store
museo	zoológico	iglesia	tienda
house	movie theater		
casa	cine		

7. museo — museum
9. cine — movie theater
10. granja — farm
11. ciudad — city
12. campo — country
13. restaurante — restaurant
14. zoológico — zoo

1. escuela — school
2. iglesia — church
3. casa — house
4. biblioteca — library
5. tienda — store
6. parque — park

Page 184

Up the Street

Circle the Spanish community-related words that you find in the word search. Write the English beside the Spanish at the bottom of the page.

Spanish Word	English	Spanish Word	English
escuela	school	tienda	store
iglesia	church	biblioteca	library
zoológico	zoo	ciudad	city
campo	country	restaurante	restaurant
casa	house	granja	farm
apartamento	apartment	cine	movie theater
museo	museum	parque	park

Page 185

Home, Sweet Home

At the bottom of each picture, copy the Spanish word.

dormitorio	vaso	cocina	casa
sala	baño	toalla	cama
estufa	televisión	lámpara	teléfono

Write the Spanish word after each room or household item.

bathroom	baño	lamp	lámpara
towel	toalla	bed	cama
television	televisión	telephone	teléfono
bedroom	dormitorio	stove	estufa
living room	sala	glass	vaso
kitchen	cocina	house	casa

Page 186

Around the House

Write the Spanish words for the clue words in the crossword puzzle.

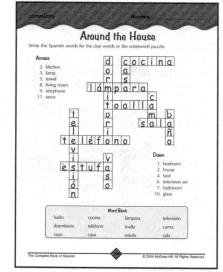

Across
2. kitchen
3. lamp
7. towel
8. living room
9. telephone
11. stove

Down
1. bedroom
2. house
4. bed
6. television set
7. bathroom
10. glass

Word Bank

baño	cocina	lámpara	televisión
dormitorio	teléfono	toalla	cama
vaso	casa	estufa	sala

Page 190

Matching Objects

Draw a line from the word to the correct picture. Color the picture.

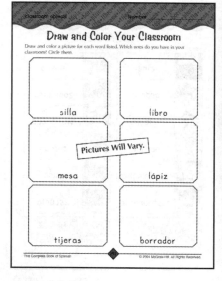

silla
libro
mesa
lápiz
tijeras
borrador

Colors Will Vary.

Page 191

Draw and Color Your Classroom

Draw and color a picture for each word listed. Which ones do you have in your classroom? Circle them.

silla	libro
mesa	lápiz
tijeras	borrador

Pictures Will Vary.

Page 192

Match Words and Pictures

Cut out pictures from a magazine and glue each picture next to the correct word.

silla
borrador
mesa
lápiz
tijeras
libro

Pictures Will Vary.

Page 193

Classroom Things

Copy each word and color the picture.

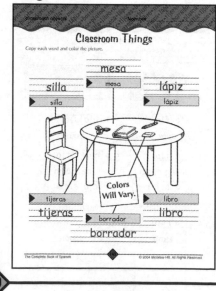

mesa
silla
lápiz
tijeras
libro
borrador

Colors Will Vary.

Answer Key

Page 194

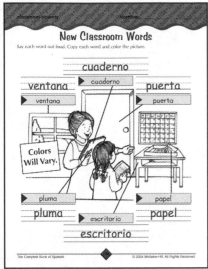

New Classroom Words

Say each word out loud. Copy each word and color the picture.

cuaderno

ventana → cuaderno → puerta

ventana · puerta

Colors Will Vary.

pluma · papel

pluma · papel

escritorio · escritorio

Page 195

Listen Carefully

Say each word out loud. Circle the picture that tells the meaning of each word.

libro
tijeras
ventana
silla
pluma
lápiz
cuaderno
mesa
puerta

Page 196

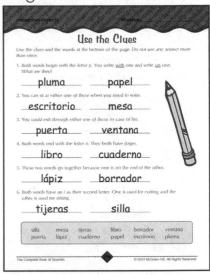

Use the Clues

Use the clues and the words at the bottom of the page. Do not use any answer more than once.

1. Both words begin with the letter p. You write with one and write on one. What are they?

pluma · papel

2. You can sit at either one of these when you need to write.

escritorio · mesa

3. You could exit through either one of these in case of fire.

puerta · ventana

4. Both words end with the letter o. They both have pages.

libro · cuaderno

5. These two words go together because one is on the end of the other.

lápiz · borrador

6. Both words have an i as their second letter. One is used for cutting and the other is used for sitting.

tijeras · silla

| silla | mesa | tijeras | libro | borrador | ventana |
| puerta | lápiz | cuaderno | papel | escritorio | pluma |

Page 197

Around the Room

In each box, copy the Spanish word for the classroom object pictured.

silla	silla	mesa	mesa
puerta	puerta	pluma	pluma
ventana	ventana	borrador	borrador
lápiz	lápiz	cuaderno	cuaderno
papel	papel	libro	libro
escritorio	escritorio	tijeras	tijeras

Write the Spanish words from above next to the English words.

window **ventana** · chair **silla** · table **mesa**
eraser **borrador** · scissors **tijeras** · door **puerta**
desk **escritorio** · pen **pluma** · notebook **cuaderno**
paper **papel** · book **libro** · pencil **lápiz**

Page 198

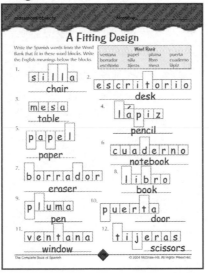

A Fitting Design

Write the Spanish words from the Word Bank that fit in these word blocks. Write the English meanings below the blocks.

Word Bank
ventana · papel · pluma · puerta
borrador · silla · libro · cuaderno
escritorio · lápiz · tijeras · mesa

1. silla — chair
2. escritorio — desk
3. mesa — table
4. lápiz — pencil
5. papel — paper
6. cuaderno — notebook
7. borrador — eraser
8. libro — book
9. pluma — pen
10. puerta — door
11. ventana — window
12. tijeras — scissors

Page 199

Where's My Pencil?

Circle the Spanish words that you find in the word search. Then write the English meaning of each word.

Spanish Word	English	Spanish Word	English
ventana	window	pluma	pen
borrador	eraser	libro	book
escritorio	desk	mesa	table
papel	paper	puerta	door
silla	chair	cuaderno	notebook
tijeras	scissors	lápiz	pencil

Page 200

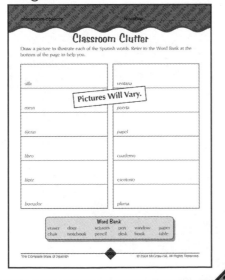

Classroom Clutter

Draw a picture to illustrate each of the Spanish words. Refer to the Word Bank at the bottom of the page to help you.

silla	ventana
mesa	puerta
tijeras	papel
libro	cuaderno
lápiz	escritorio
borrador	pluma

Pictures Will Vary.

Word Bank
eraser · door · scissors · pen · window · paper
chair · notebook · pencil · desk · book · table

Page 201

Show and Tell

Write the Spanish for each clue in the crossword puzzle.

Across
1. notebook
5. scissors
7. pen
8. eraser
10. pencil
11. table
12. chair

Down
2. desk
3. window
4. book
6. door
9. paper

cuaderno · ventana · tijeras · pluma · borrador · lápiz · mesa · silla · escritorio

Word Bank
escritorio · mesa · libro · silla · tijeras · puerta
lápiz · ventana · borrador · cuaderno · papel · pluma

The Complete Book of Spanish

Page 202

classroom objects · · · · · · · · Nombre _____

Pencil and Paper

Copy the following sentences in Spanish. Then, write the English meanings.

1. El libro es rojo. __El libro es rojo.__
   __The book is red.__
2. La silla es de color café. __La silla es de color café.__
   __The chair is brown.__
3. El cuaderno es morado. __El cuaderno es morado.__
   __The notebook is purple.__
4. La mesa es verde. __La mesa es verde.__
   __The table is green.__
5. El lápiz es rosado. __El lápiz es rosado.__
   __The pencil is pink.__
6. El borrador es amarillo. __El borrador es amarillo.__
   __The eraser is yellow.__
7. La ventana es azul. __La ventana es azul.__
   __The window is blue.__
8. El escritorio es anaranjado. __El escritorio es anaranjado.__
   __The desk is orange.__
9. El papel es blanco. __El papel es blanco.__
   __The paper is white.__

The Complete Book of Spanish   © 2004 McGraw-Hill. All Rights Reserved.

Page 320

final review · · · · · · · · Nombre _____

Final Review

For each English word given, write the Spanish word with the same meaning. Use the number of blanks as clues. Can you find the hidden word spelled down in each list?

four	c u a t r o	mother	m a d r e
hand	m a n o	kitchen	c o c i n a
blue	a z u l	clean	l i m p i o
fruit	f r u t a	thirty	t r e i n t a
chair	s i l l a	paint	p i n t e n
church	i g l e s i a	friend (m)	a m i g o
hello	h o l a	to eat	c o m e r
boots	b o t a s		

the letter h	h a c h e	Hidden Words
Saturday	s á b a d o	1. amarillo
horse	c a b a l l o	2. domingo
milk	l e c h e	3. calcetines
black	n e g r o	
you (formal)	u s t e d	
goodbye	a d i ó s	
store	t i e n d a	
teacher (female)	m a e s t r a	
hat	s o m b r e r o	

The Complete Book of Spanish   320   © 2004 McGraw-Hill. All Rights Reserved.